HANDWORK
SKILLS & THEMES

First published in Great Britain 1983 by
Belair Publications Limited,
P.O. Box 12,
Twickenham TW1 2QL
England.
Reprinted 1984, 1985, 1986,
1987 (twice), 1990 and 1994

© 1981 DAVID E. CORNEY

Printed in Hong Kong by
World Print Limited

ISBN 0 947882 00 6

Published in Australia by
Belair Publications Pty. Ltd,
73 Madison Drive,
Adamstown Heights,
N.S.W. 2289, Australia.

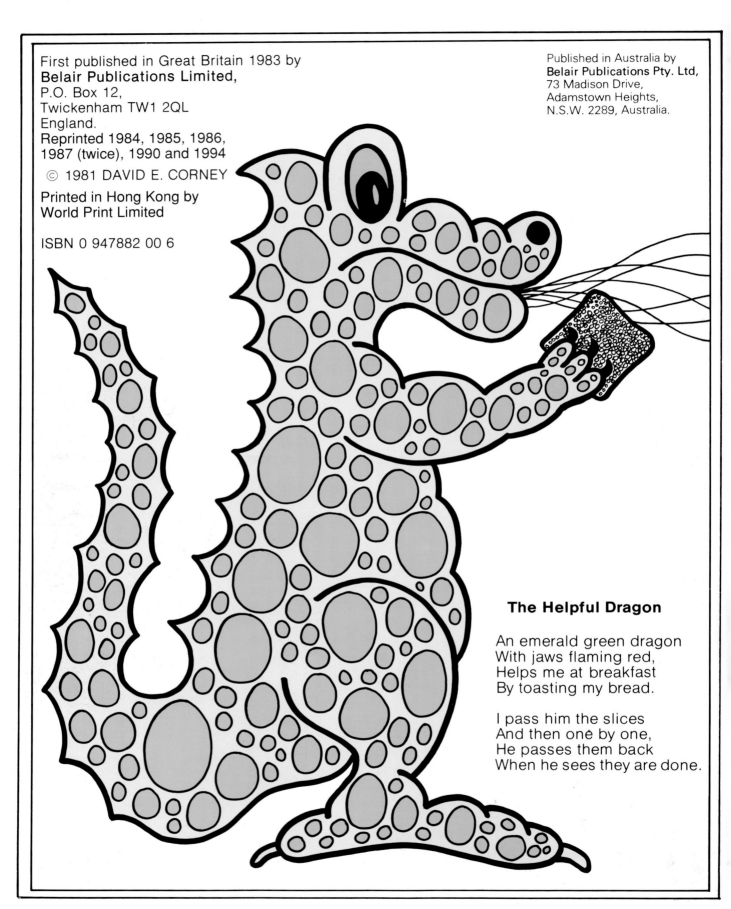

The Helpful Dragon

An emerald green dragon
With jaws flaming red,
Helps me at breakfast
By toasting my bread.

I pass him the slices
And then one by one,
He passes them back
When he sees they are done.

HANDWORK
SKILLS & THEMES

DAVID E. CORNEY

Senior Lecturer — Newcastle College of Advanced Education, N.S.W., Australia

ABOVE: This "Springtime" theme combines a wide range of skills and processes.

BELOW: Tufting has been used to represent the sheep and her spring lamb.

INTRODUCTION

Just as the ability to read and write or the ability to add, subtract, multiply and divide is based on the progressive acquisition of related skills, so too is the child's ability to create or construct dependent on the acquisition of fundamental manipulative skills and processes.

It may well be claimed that many of these skills are innate, and while it is widely recognised that young children enjoy a high level of innate creativity, the children's ability to express their ideas is frequently frustrated by their lack of knowledge about the materials they are using or the skills which will enable them to give form to the information at hand.

Handwork Skills and Themes is essentially a book of ideas and procedures which will assist teachers in the presentation of the basic manipulative skills and at the same time offer suggestions of subject areas and themes to which these skills can be related.

Overall, the book is intended to facilitate the integration of the total learning process, a process in which ideas, skills, materials and individual creativity all contribute to the education of the child.

It is anticipated that the contents of Handwork Skills and Themes will find application in both Infant and Primary grades. In Infant grades the skills will be introduced and developed, while in Primary grades, children with a higher level of manual dexterity and inventiveness will find new and more challenging applications for the basic manipulative processes.

For both the teacher and the children it is the author's intention that the activities should provide mutual enjoyment and a sense of achievement through participation.

IN APPRECIATION

The ideas and activities presented in Handwork Skills and Themes represent the combined talents and efforts of many people.

To the teachers who have so generously granted permission to photograph examples of work prepared by children under their guidance, I record my sincere appreciation.

For permission to reproduce photographs included in this book I am indebted to the Staff of the Infants' Departments of Belair Primary School, Belmont Primary School, Charlestown East Primary School, Gateshead West Primary School, Gunnedah South Primary School, Lindfield Demonstration School, New Lambton Primary School, New Lambton South Primary School, North Sydney Demonstration School and Windale Primary School.

To my students at Newcastle College of Advanced Education who enthusiastically contributed through the development of new ideas and experimental projects and to my colleague Ross Owen, for the use of material which has resulted from his professional expertise, I extend my grateful appreciation.

David E. Comey

Newcastle, New South Wales,
Australia

IDENTIFYING THE MANIPULATIVE SKILLS   THEME: Birds

CUTTING

Diagonally fold a square of cardboard then fold cut the standing rooster.

CHIPPING

Add chipping to body areas.

CRUMPLING

Apply crumpling to create a 3D effect on the egg or body of the chick.

CURLING

Curl strips and glue to form bird mobile.

Curl tail feathers and glue to body.

FOLDING

Head

Body

Cut

Fold the head and body to make bluebirds.

FRINGING

Use fringing to represent the Emu's feathers.

Fringe clumps of grass.

Fringe a bottlebrush.

PLEATING

Pleating is a series of parallel folds in alternate directions.

ROLLING

Roll from corner to corner.

TEARING

Control tearing with thumbs and forefingers.

TUFTING

Gather paper around pencil then press onto glue.

TWISTING

WEAVING

Finish weavers on the back surface to leave a regular pattern on the front.

Cutting is a skill common to all handwork activities, therefore time spent establishing correct procedures in the early stages of a child's development will generate confidence and competence as the basic skill of cutting is applied to more complex tasks.

Cutting

It's fun to use my scissors,
And see the sharp blades snip,
Around a picture that I've drawn
Of me, or of a ship.

I hold the scissors carefully,
So they will not slip,
And cut around the outline,
Snip, snip, snip.

Scissors are so useful,
They cut so many things,
Like apples for an apple tree,
Or feathers for birds' wings.

So when you're using scissors
At home, at play, or school
Always use them carefully,
That's a golden rule.

After children have mastered cutting simple outlines, more demanding shapes can be introduced. Have the children trace the outline of their outstretched hand on a sheet of paper, then, after cutting around the outline, make the resulting shape into a new form.

Rooster

Cock-a-doodle-doo,
A rooster greets
the dawn.
Cock-a-doodle-doo,
Sunrise heralds
morn.

- Cut a rooster shape.
- Children print coloured handprints.
- Allow prints to dry.
- Cut prints around the outline and glue them to the body to represent feathers, comb, etc.

Create a design based on a study of ants.
Cut around the outline and display on a colour of
strong contrast.

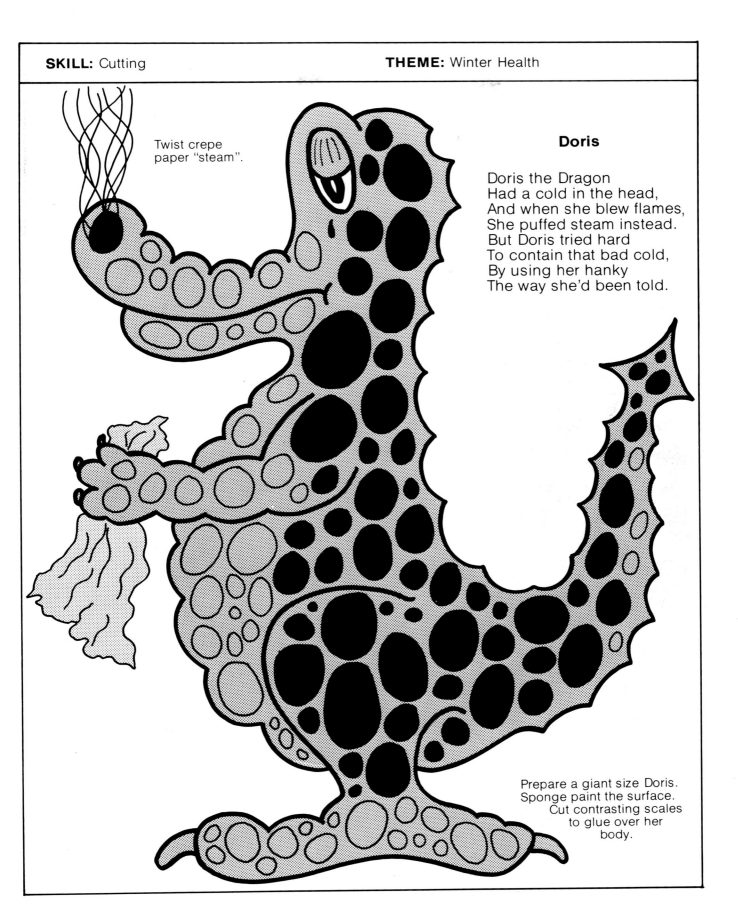

Twist crepe
paper "steam".

Doris

Doris the Dragon
Had a cold in the head,
And when she blew flames,
She puffed steam instead.
But Doris tried hard
To contain that bad cold,
By using her hanky
The way she'd been told.

Prepare a giant size Doris.
Sponge paint the surface.
Cut contrasting scales
to glue over her
body.

SKILL: Fold cutting plus selected paper skills.   **THEME:** Children of the World

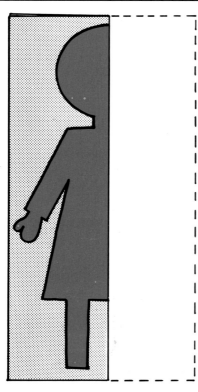

Fold cut basic form of
each figure.

Apply various paper skills, fabric scraps, paint or printing
techniques to represent the different forms of dress.

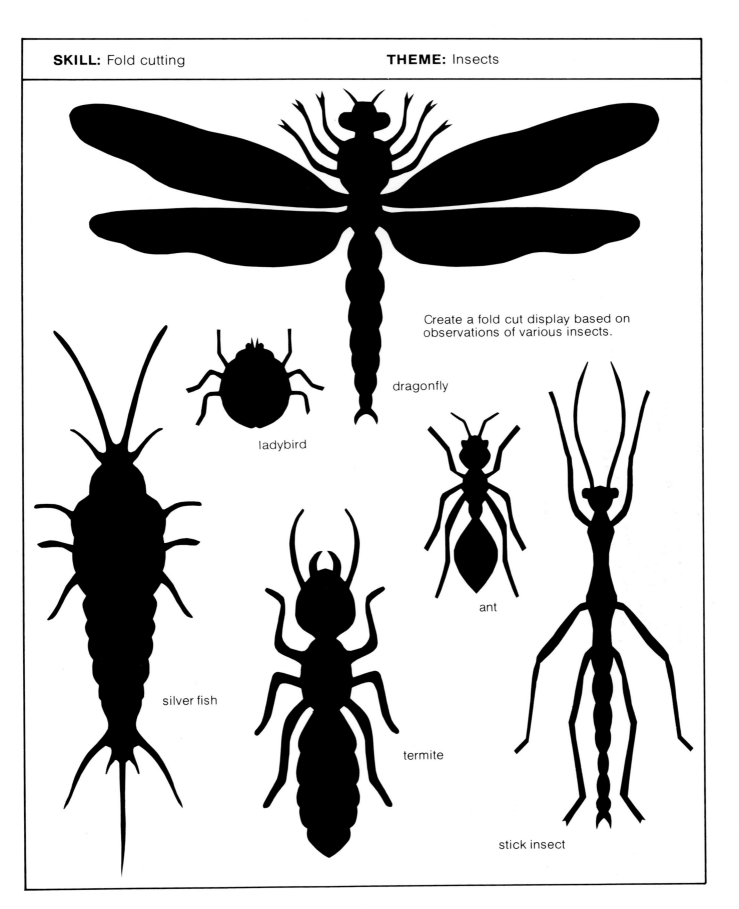

Create a fold cut display based on observations of various insects.

dragonfly

ladybird

silver fish

termite

ant

stick insect

Fold a strip of paper several times, then pencil the outline lightly on the outside surface. Part of the outline MUST touch the edge. When cutting the outline, this part is NOT cut away and acts as a hinge in joining the adjacent units.

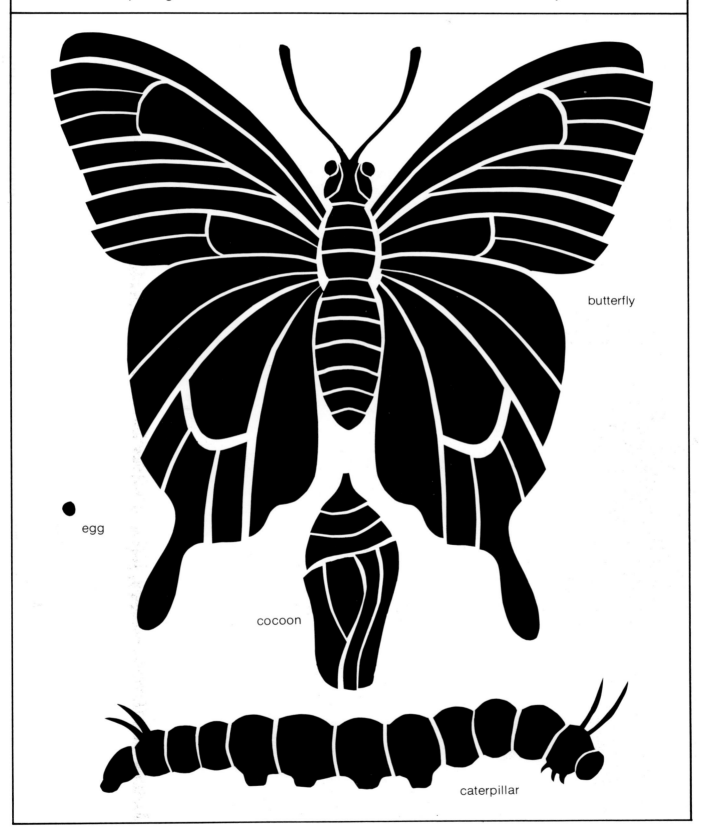

butterfly

egg

cocoon

caterpillar

Children in Kindergarten have used a variety of skills to represent the characters of stories they have been reading with their teacher.

This bowl of colourful daffodils provides an attractive spring display. The centres of the daffodils have been made from single egg carton units glued to the petal shapes.

Using the skills shown on page 78, these giant flowers are ideal for adding a touch of springtime colour to a classroom wall or display area. Centres can be filled with tufting, crumpling or a circle of painted cardboard.

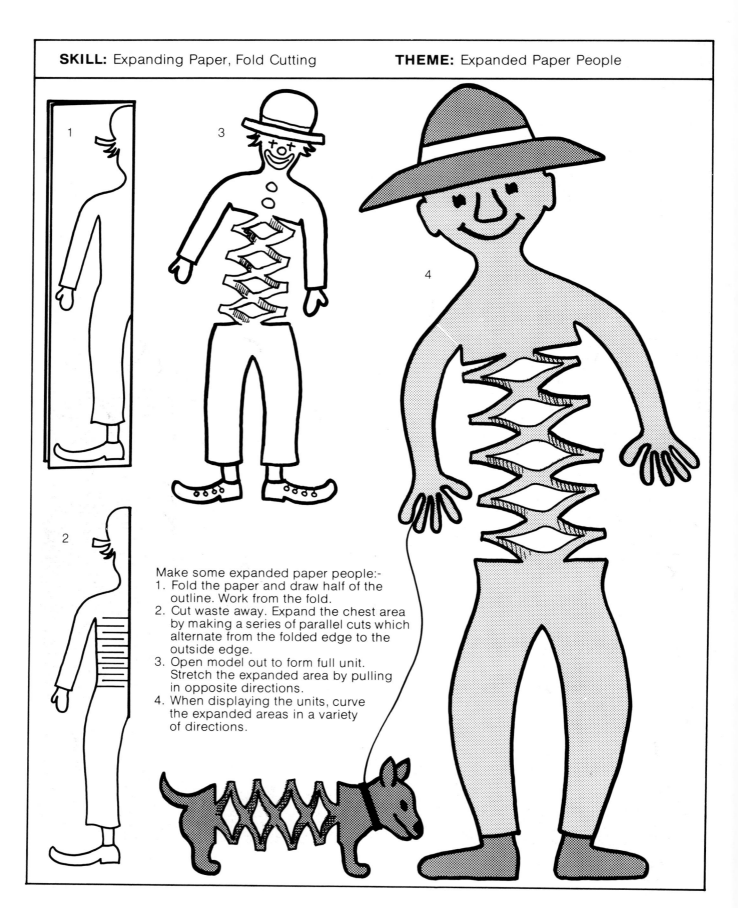

Make some expanded paper people:-
1. Fold the paper and draw half of the outline. Work from the fold.
2. Cut waste away. Expand the chest area by making a series of parallel cuts which alternate from the folded edge to the outside edge.
3. Open model out to form full unit. Stretch the expanded area by pulling in opposite directions.
4. When displaying the units, curve the expanded areas in a variety of directions.

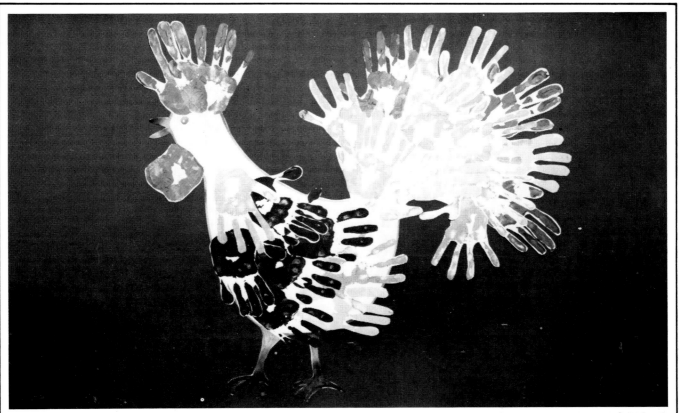

Hand prints, cut to their outline, form the flowing feathers and comb of the rooster. Glue the handprints to a rooster shaped base. Ref. page 9.

Meet the "Colour Creatures". Fold painted areas of bright colours have been cut to the outline to form the faces. Body and limb details have been painted onto the background.

Yellow Duck

I think it is a stroke of luck,
That I hatched out a yellow duck.
Yellow coat and yellow shoes,
Just to wander where I choose.

Cover head and body circles with chipping, add beak, etc. Crumple rocks and reeds.

THEME: The Merry Mice

The Merry Mice

The merry mice hide in their holes,
And sleep the day away,
But when the house is still at night
Those rogues come out to play.

They climb up to the pantry shelf
And sample all they please,
They taste the cake and drink some milk,
Then nibble bread and cheese.

But if, by chance, they hear the cat,
Their feast is quickly done.
They scamper off to hide themselves,
As fast as they can run.

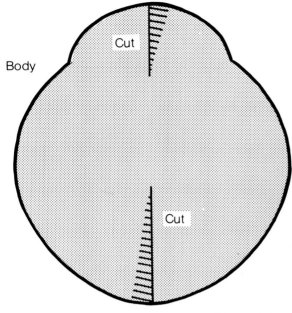

Body

Cut

Cut

Cut body of ladybird. To form a 3D model, cut lines shown, glue and overlap shaded area.

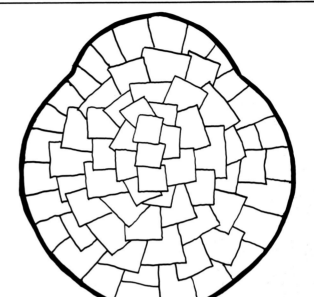

Cover body with chipped paper.

Twist legs and glue under edge of body.
Add black spots and eyes.

Ladybirds

If you should see a Ladybird
Out basking in the sun,
Pass by it very quietly,
Don't bounce or skip or run.
For ladybirds are gentle things,
Most welcome on a farm,
They feed on tiny insects,
And really do no harm.
Their coat is golden orange,
With black spots on their wings,
And tiny legs to creep about,
They're very timid things.

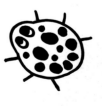

  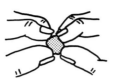 

Use larger squares for larger units.

Crumpling is a skill which produces a three dimensional appearance when the crumpled paper balls are glued onto a flat surface.

Children should be encouraged to work with their fingers and thumbs, rather than rolling the paper between the palms of their hands, as the former practice facilitates greater manipulative development.

When gluing the crumpled balls, use a strong adhesive such as P.V.A. Spread the glue over all or part of the area and press the crumpled paper onto the wet glue.

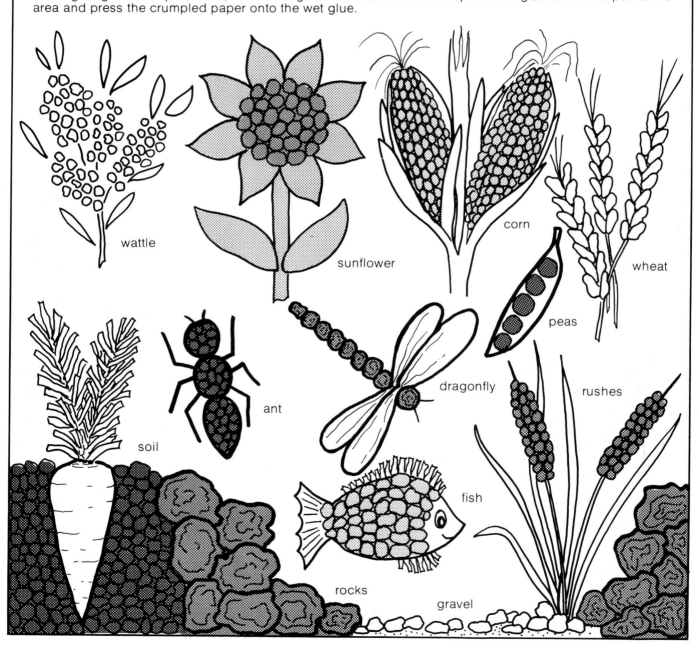

wattle

sunflower

corn

wheat

peas

soil

ant

dragonfly

rushes

fish

rocks

gravel

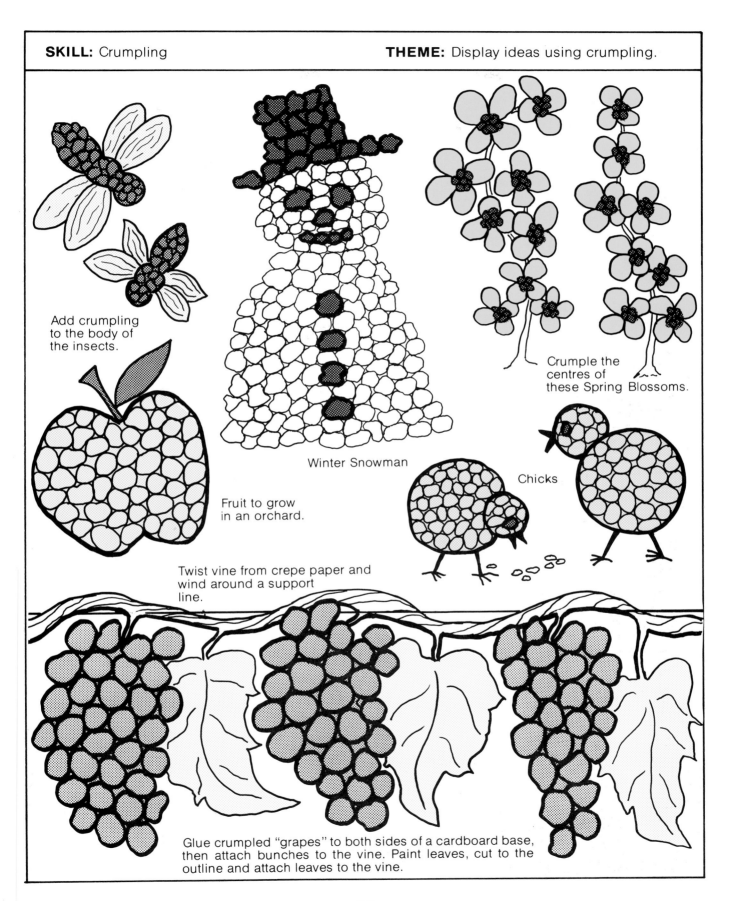

Add crumpling to the body of the insects.

Winter Snowman

Crumple the centres of these Spring Blossoms.

Fruit to grow in an orchard.

Chicks

Twist vine from crepe paper and wind around a support line.

Glue crumpled "grapes" to both sides of a cardboard base, then attach bunches to the vine. Paint leaves, cut to the outline and attach leaves to the vine.

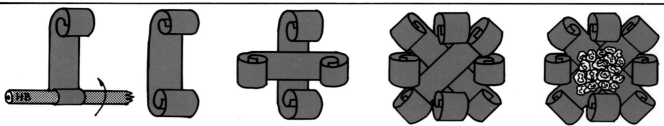

Cut four strips of paper, then using a pencil, curl both ends of each strip towards the centre. Glue two strips together at right angles, then the other two at 45° as shown above - fill the centre of the flower with crumpling or tufting.

1. Display individual units in the form of a flowering vine. Twist a crepe paper stem, add finger painted or printed leaves. Use masking tape loops to attach flowers to vine.

2. Roll stems, to which flowers and leaves are glued. Support flowers in a block of styrofoam. Decorate as a window box.

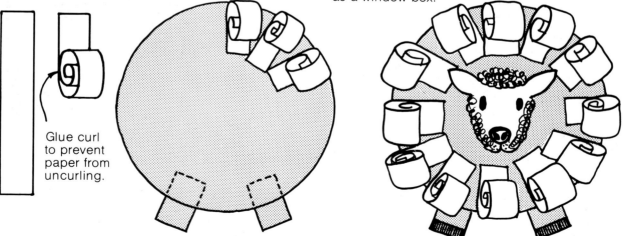

Glue curl to prevent paper from uncurling.

Make a "Springtime" display of woolly sheep. Cut a circle from light cardboard, then add legs and one or two rows of paper curls. Glue the sheep's head in the centre of the curls.

Tufting

Crepe paper hat.

Many interesting and varied displays can be created by applying a range of skills to the surfaces of a cardboard carton. The actual size of the carton can extend from a clean milk carton to a large packing carton, however the most effective units result when large models are attempted. Where height is required in the model, this can be achieved by gluing, or simply standing, one carton on top of another.

Large areas should be painted with appropriate background colours before the detailed skills are applied. Styrofoam shapes are handy for eyes, nose and other details which need to stand out from the main surface.

SKILL: Folding - Corner to corner   **THEME:** Poem - Mother Hen

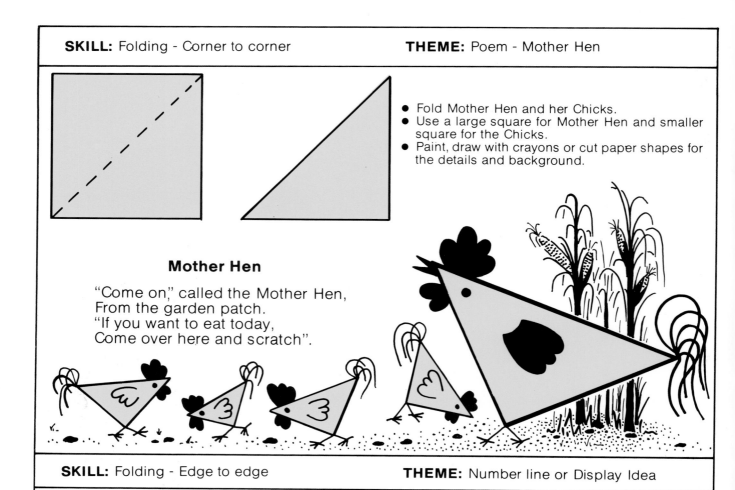

- Fold Mother Hen and her Chicks.
- Use a large square for Mother Hen and smaller square for the Chicks.
- Paint, draw with crayons or cut paper shapes for the details and background.

Mother Hen

"Come on," called the Mother Hen,
From the garden patch.
"If you want to eat today,
Come over here and scratch".

SKILL: Folding - Edge to edge   **THEME:** Number line or Display Idea

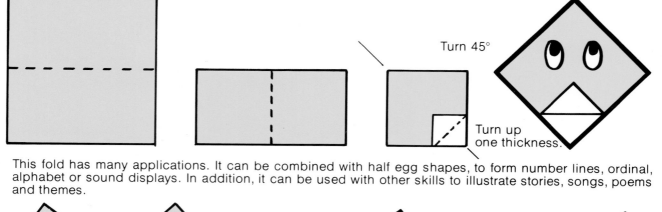

Turn 45°

Turn up one thickness.

This fold has many applications. It can be combined with half egg shapes, to form number lines, ordinal, alphabet or sound displays. In addition, it can be used with other skills to illustrate stories, songs, poems and themes.

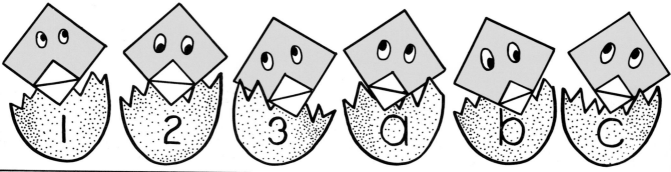

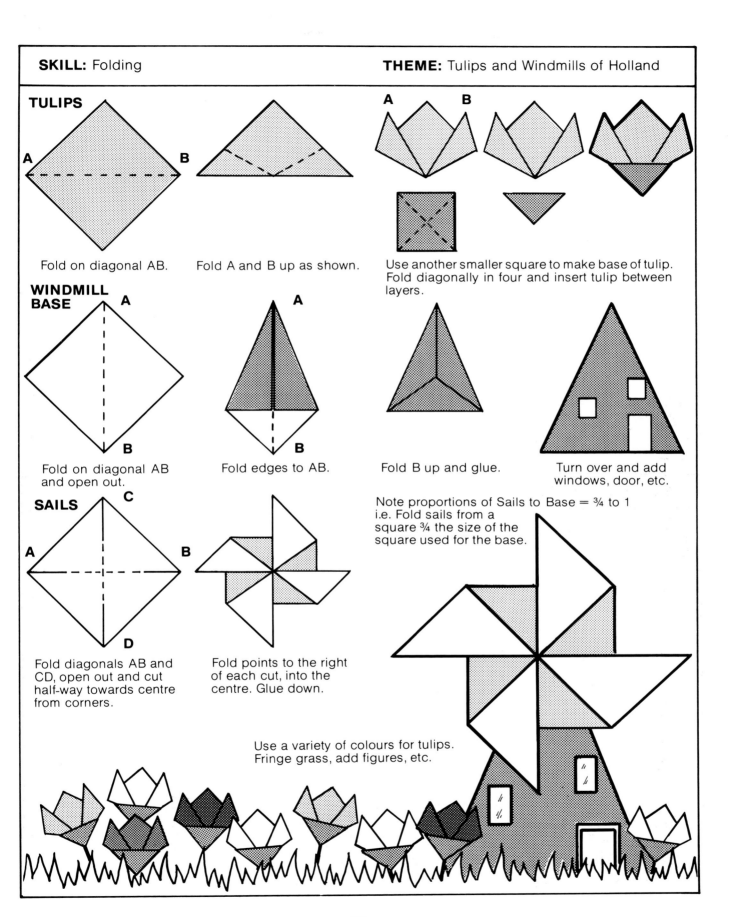

TULIPS

Fold on diagonal AB.

Fold A and B up as shown.

Use another smaller square to make base of tulip. Fold diagonally in four and insert tulip between layers.

WINDMILL BASE

Fold on diagonal AB and open out.

Fold edges to AB.

Fold B up and glue.

Turn over and add windows, door, etc.

SAILS

Fold diagonals AB and CD, open out and cut half-way towards centre from corners.

Fold points to the right of each cut, into the centre. Glue down.

Note proportions of Sails to Base = ¾ to 1 i.e. Fold sails from a square ¾ the size of the square used for the base.

Use a variety of colours for tulips. Fringe grass, add figures, etc.

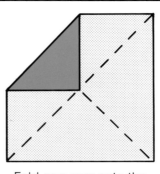

Fold diagonally to locate centre.

Fold one corner to the centre.

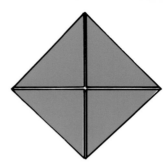

Repeat this fold for the other corners.

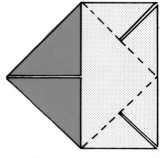

Open two adjacent corners and cut from corners to fold line.

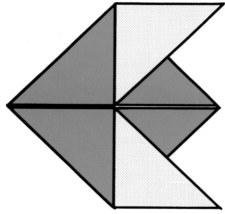

Fold the two inner halves back into the centre. Glue all folds down. Turn over to add detail.

Alternate method of forming fish.

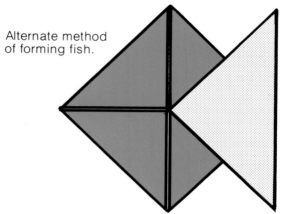

Fold the two outer halves back into the centre. Glue all folds down. Turn over to add detail.

The Stream

Over in the stream,
By the big gum tree,
Swims old Mother Fish,
And her school of thirty-three.

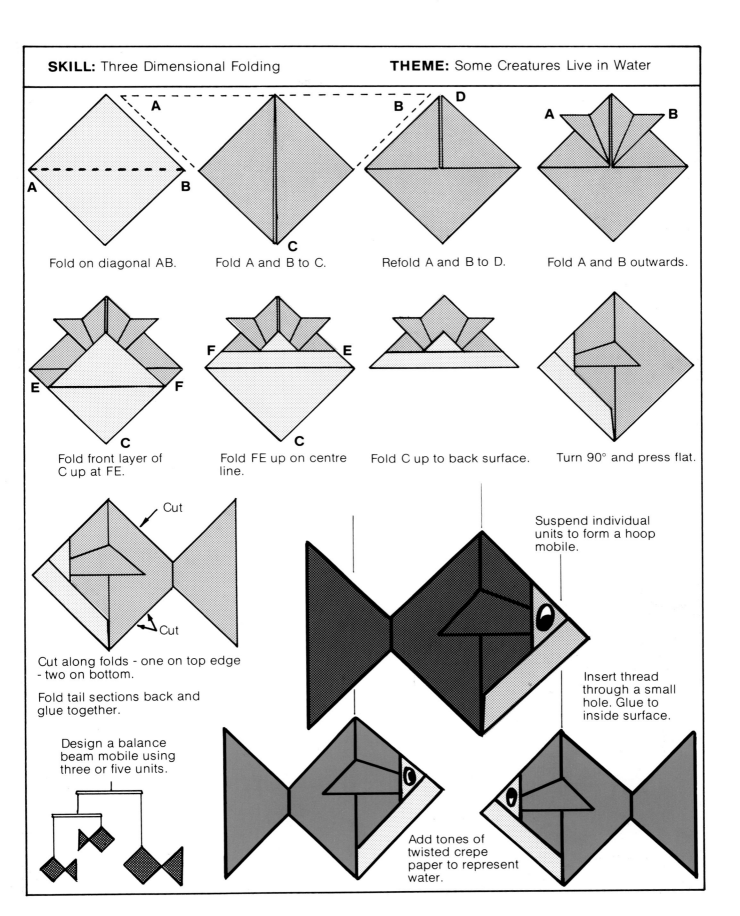

Fold on diagonal AB.

Fold A and B to C.

Refold A and B to D.

Fold A and B outwards.

Fold front layer of C up at FE.

Fold FE up on centre line.

Fold C up to back surface.

Turn 90° and press flat.

Cut along folds - one on top edge - two on bottom.

Fold tail sections back and glue together.

Design a balance beam mobile using three or five units.

Suspend individual units to form a hoop mobile.

Insert thread through a small hole. Glue to inside surface.

Add tones of twisted crepe paper to represent water.

31

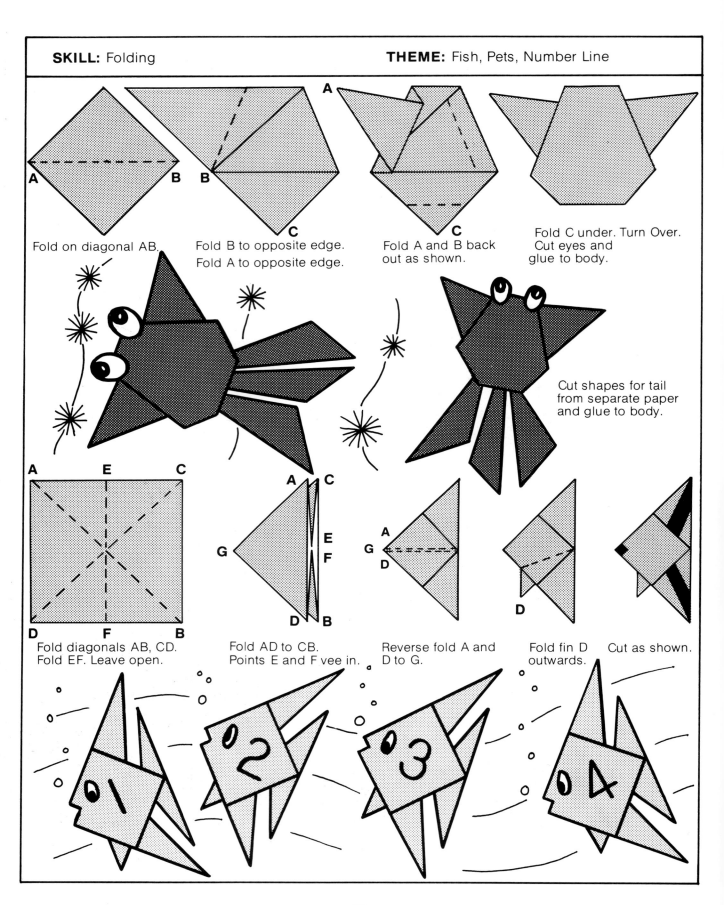

Fold on diagonal AB.

Fold B to opposite edge.
Fold A to opposite edge.

Fold A and B back out as shown.

Fold C under. Turn Over.
Cut eyes and glue to body.

Cut shapes for tail from separate paper and glue to body.

Fold diagonals AB, CD.
Fold EF. Leave open.

Fold AD to CB.
Points E and F vee in.

Reverse fold A and D to G.

Fold fin D outwards.   Cut as shown.

A combination of two and three dimensional skills has been used to form this display based on the theme of Halloween.

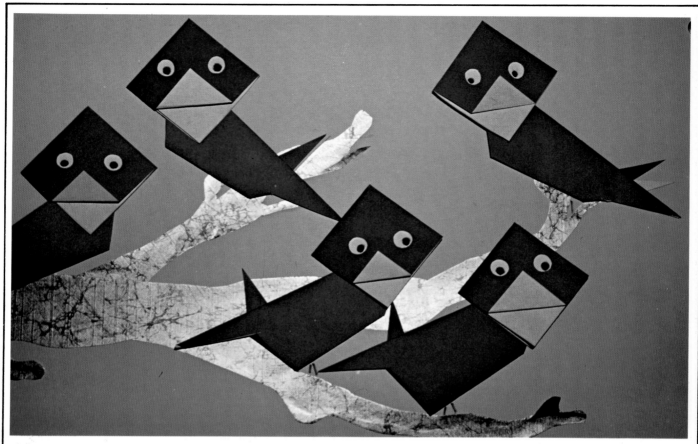

ABOVE: This simple paper fold provides an easy method of making bluebirds.

BELOW: As an effective group activity, five or six children can design a colourful bird. Using a variety of paper skills the surface of each bird is enriched with colour and texture, then the collective display is formed by arranging the birds in an aviary. Use a plain background to heighten the contrast of the display.

ABOVE: A variety of scrap materials has been used to make this selection of mouth watering cakes. Integrate the children's work in numeracy with the Cake Shop through appropriate number problems.

BELOW: Paper folding has been combined with other skills to form this bowl of fish.

How many fish live in this bowl?

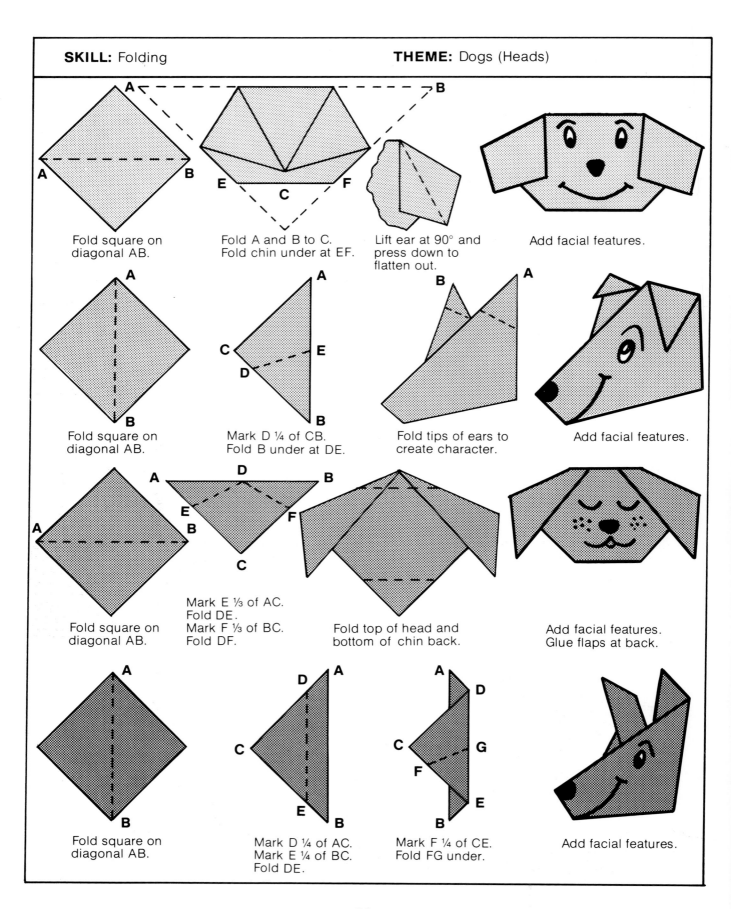

Fold square on diagonal AB.

Fold A and B to C. Fold chin under at EF.

Lift ear at 90° and press down to flatten out.

Add facial features.

Fold square on diagonal AB.

Mark D ¼ of CB. Fold B under at DE.

Fold tips of ears to create character.

Add facial features.

Fold square on diagonal AB.

Mark E ⅓ of AC. Fold DE. Mark F ⅓ of BC. Fold DF.

Fold top of head and bottom of chin back.

Add facial features. Glue flaps at back.

Fold square on diagonal AB.

Mark D ¼ of AC. Mark E ¼ of BC. Fold DE.

Mark F ¼ of CE. Fold FG under.

Add facial features.

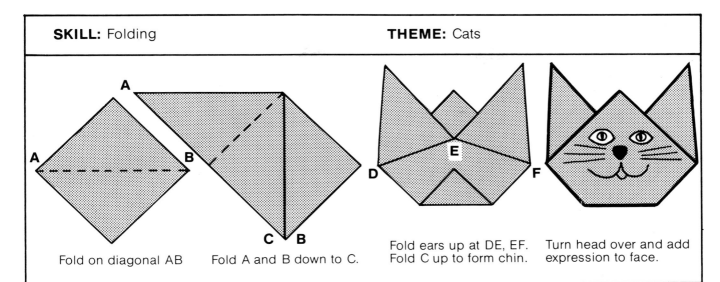

Fold on diagonal AB   Fold A and B down to C.   Fold ears up at DE, EF.   Turn head over and add
                                              Fold C up to form chin.   expression to face.

Use the folds shown on this and other pages to illustrate the poems set out below.
Encourage children to paint or draw on details. As an alternate method of representation, children can fold
heads and paint body shapes or simply paint all of their ideas.

Cats

Cats sleep anywhere,
In the sunshine,
On a chair.
Perched upon a garden tub,
In the shade of your best shrub.
Curled up in a cardboard box,
In the washing with your socks.
Top of carport, near the edge,
Huddled on a window ledge.
Never seem to have a care,
Busy sleeping - anywhere.

Puppies

Puppies are furry,
And wiggly and cuddly,
And on rainy days
Their feet get mud puddly.

They chew and strew things
In puppy dog pranks,
And waggle their way
Out of scoldings and spanks.

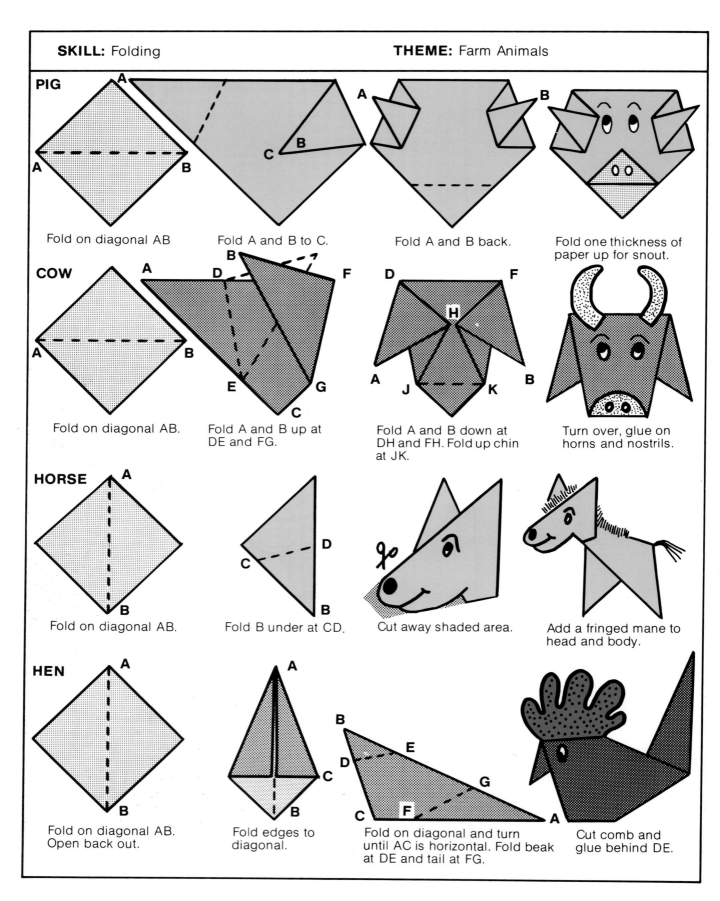

SKILL: Folding   **THEME:** Farm Animals

PIG

Fold on diagonal AB

Fold A and B to C.

Fold A and B back.

Fold one thickness of paper up for snout.

COW

Fold on diagonal AB.

Fold A and B up at DE and FG.

Fold A and B down at DH and FH. Fold up chin at JK.

Turn over, glue on horns and nostrils.

HORSE

Fold on diagonal AB.

Fold B under at CD.

Cut away shaded area.

Add a fringed mane to head and body.

HEN

Fold on diagonal AB. Open back out.

Fold edges to diagonal.

Fold on diagonal and turn until AC is horizontal. Fold beak at DE and tail at FG.

Cut comb and glue behind DE.

38

The four shapes shown below represent the positions of standing, sitting, running and lying. Body shapes can be combined with most of the heads set out on the previous pages.

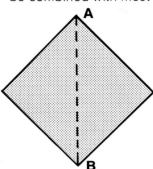

Fold on diagonal AB

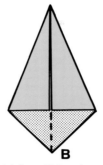

Fold edge AC to AB.
Fold edge AD to AB.

Fold flap B back under and glue down.

Add an animal head.

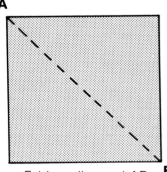

Fold on diagonal AB

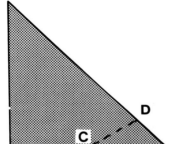

Fold on CD for tail.

Cut shaded area.

Add an animal head.

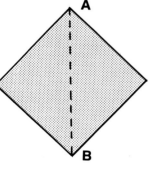

Fold on diagonal AB

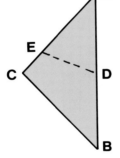

Fold DE. Note CE is about ¼ CA.

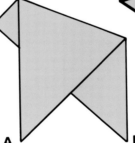

By spacing points A and B, different types of movement can be implied: Close = slow action, Apart = running.

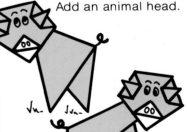

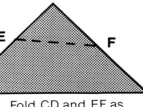

Fold on diagonal AB

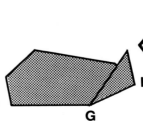

Fold CD and EF as shown to give proportions of body.

Fold GH up for tail.

Add an animal head.

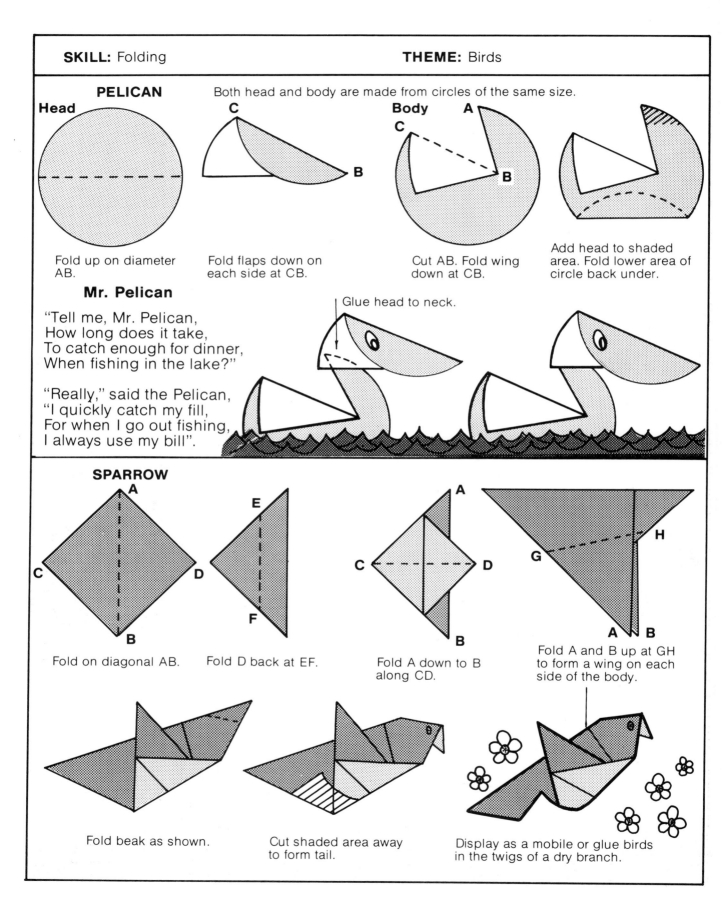

PELICAN

Head

Both head and body are made from circles of the same size.

Body

Fold up on diameter AB.

Fold flaps down on each side at CB.

Cut AB. Fold wing down at CB.

Add head to shaded area. Fold lower area of circle back under.

Mr. Pelican

"Tell me, Mr. Pelican,
How long does it take,
To catch enough for dinner,
When fishing in the lake?"

"Really," said the Pelican,
"I quickly catch my fill,
For when I go out fishing,
I always use my bill".

Glue head to neck.

SPARROW

Fold on diagonal AB.

Fold D back at EF.

Fold A down to B along CD.

Fold A and B up at GH to form a wing on each side of the body.

Fold beak as shown.

Cut shaded area away to form tail.

Display as a mobile or glue birds in the twigs of a dry branch.

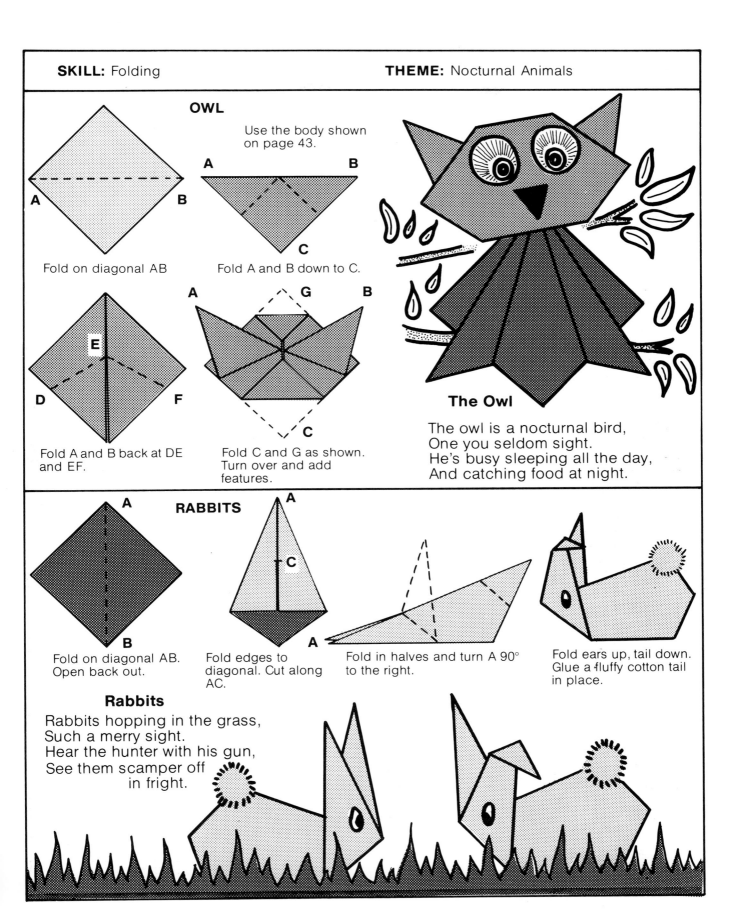

SKILL: Folding   **THEME:** Nocturnal Animals

OWL

Use the body shown on page 43.

A ____ B

Fold on diagonal AB

A   B
C

Fold A and B down to C.

E
D   F

Fold A and B back at DE and EF.

A   G   B
C

Fold C and G as shown. Turn over and add features.

The Owl

The owl is a nocturnal bird,
One you seldom sight.
He's busy sleeping all the day,
And catching food at night.

RABBITS

A
B

Fold on diagonal AB. Open back out.

A
C
A

Fold edges to diagonal. Cut along AC.

Fold in halves and turn A 90° to the right.

Fold ears up, tail down. Glue a fluffy cotton tail in place.

Rabbits

Rabbits hopping in the grass,
Such a merry sight.
Hear the hunter with his gun,
See them scamper off
in fright.

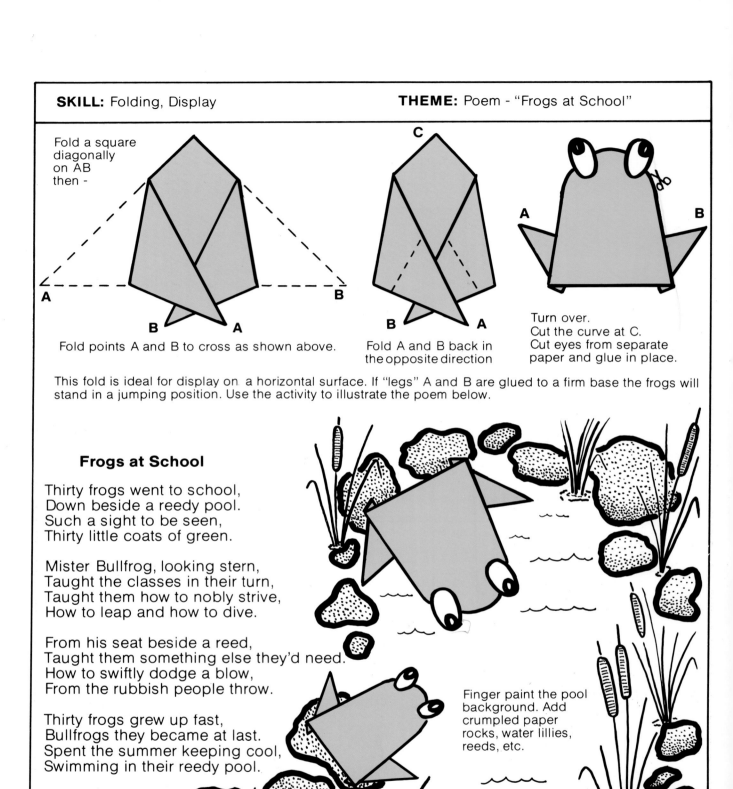

Fold a square diagonally on AB then -

Fold points A and B to cross as shown above.

Fold A and B back in the opposite direction

Turn over.
Cut the curve at C.
Cut eyes from separate paper and glue in place.

This fold is ideal for display on a horizontal surface. If "legs" A and B are glued to a firm base the frogs will stand in a jumping position. Use the activity to illustrate the poem below.

Frogs at School

Thirty frogs went to school,
Down beside a reedy pool.
Such a sight to be seen,
Thirty little coats of green.

Mister Bullfrog, looking stern,
Taught the classes in their turn,
Taught them how to nobly strive,
How to leap and how to dive.

From his seat beside a reed,
Taught them something else they'd need.
How to swiftly dodge a blow,
From the rubbish people throw.

Thirty frogs grew up fast,
Bullfrogs they became at last.
Spent the summer keeping cool,
Swimming in their reedy pool.

Finger paint the pool background. Add crumpled paper rocks, water lillies, reeds, etc.

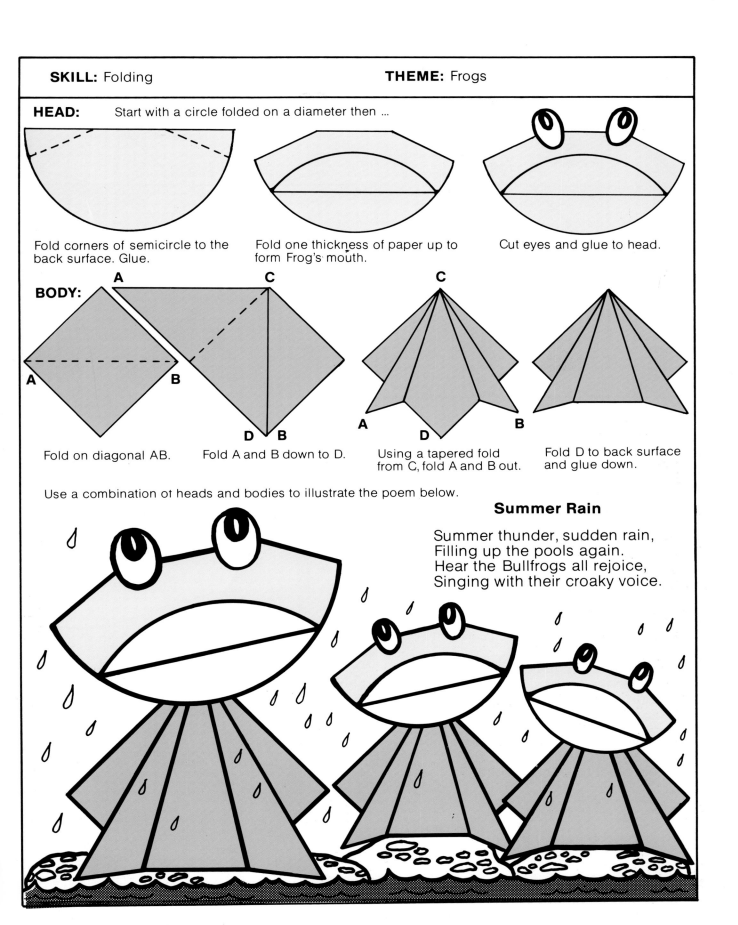

HEAD: Start with a circle folded on a diameter then ...

Fold corners of semicircle to the back surface. Glue.

Fold one thickness of paper up to form Frog's mouth.

Cut eyes and glue to head.

BODY:

A   C

A   B

D B

C

A D B

Fold on diagonal AB.

Fold A and B down to D.

Using a tapered fold from C, fold A and B out.

Fold D to back surface and glue down.

Use a combination of heads and bodies to illustrate the poem below.

Summer Rain

Summer thunder, sudden rain,
Filling up the pools again.
Hear the Bullfrogs all rejoice,
Singing with their croaky voice.

43

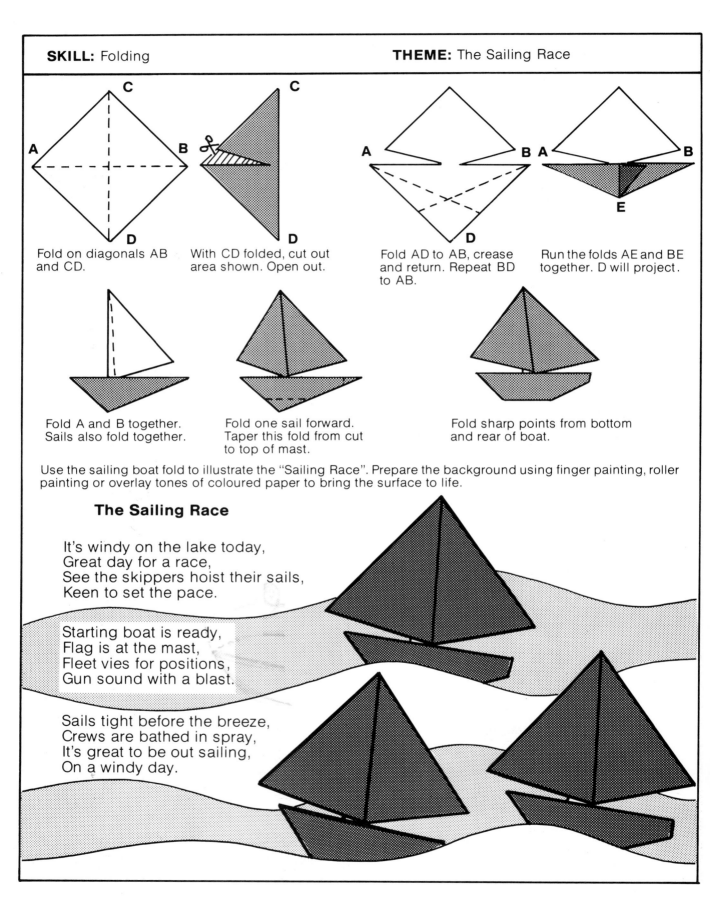

Fold on diagonals AB and CD.

With CD folded, cut out area shown. Open out.

Fold AD to AB, crease and return. Repeat BD to AB.

Run the folds AE and BE together. D will project.

Fold A and B together. Sails also fold together.

Fold one sail forward. Taper this fold from cut to top of mast.

Fold sharp points from bottom and rear of boat.

Use the sailing boat fold to illustrate the "Sailing Race". Prepare the background using finger painting, roller painting or overlay tones of coloured paper to bring the surface to life.

The Sailing Race

It's windy on the lake today,
Great day for a race,
See the skippers hoist their sails,
Keen to set the pace.

Starting boat is ready,
Flag is at the mast,
Fleet vies for positions,
Gun sound with a blast.

Sails tight before the breeze,
Crews are bathed in spray,
It's great to be out sailing,
On a windy day.

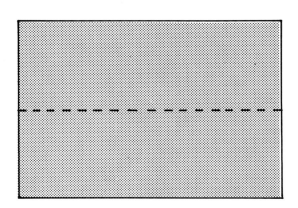

Start with an oblong 9cm x 12cm or one of similar proportion. Fold in half.

With the fold to the top, fold each end over at 45°, crease and open back out again.

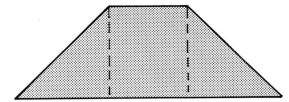

Tuck the area above the crease back inside the main area by reversing the fold. Do this at each end. Glue seams.

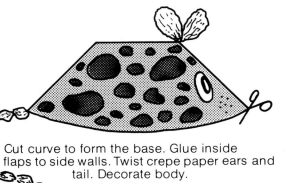

Cut curve to form the base. Glue inside flaps to side walls. Twist crepe paper ears and tail. Decorate body.

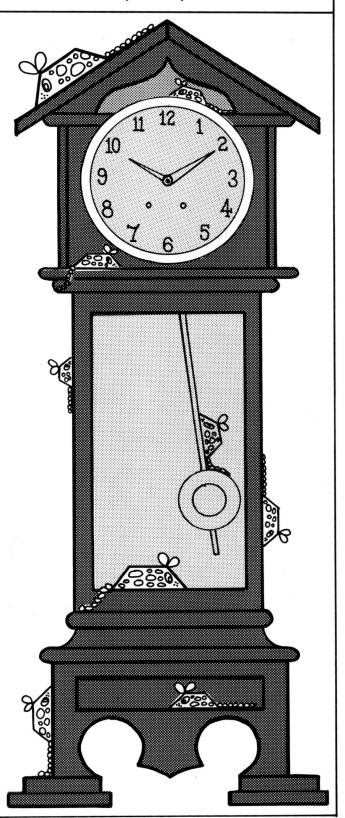

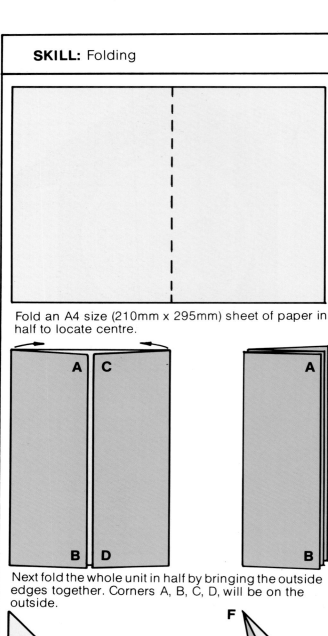

Fold an A4 size (210mm x 295mm) sheet of paper in half to locate centre.

Next fold the whole unit in half by bringing the outside edges together. Corners A, B, C, D, will be on the outside.

Cut as shown above. Fold edges on top surface back on a line from end of cut E to points F and G. Turn over and repeat on bottom surface.

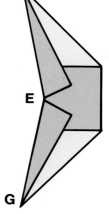

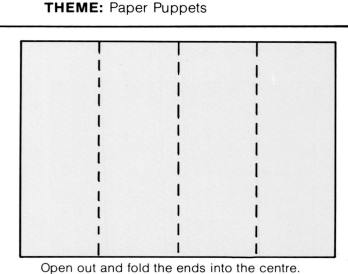

Open out and fold the ends into the centre.

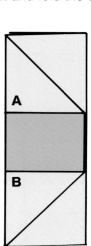
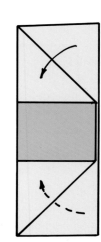

Fold the single thicknesses at A and B down at 45°, repeat with single thickness on back surface. Fold double thickness forwards at top and backwards at the bottom. Glue all flaps.

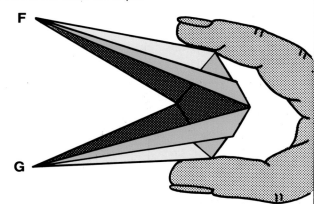

Squeeze points F and G together to form mouth of puppet. Use as a hand puppet, shown above, or add a neck as shown opposite.

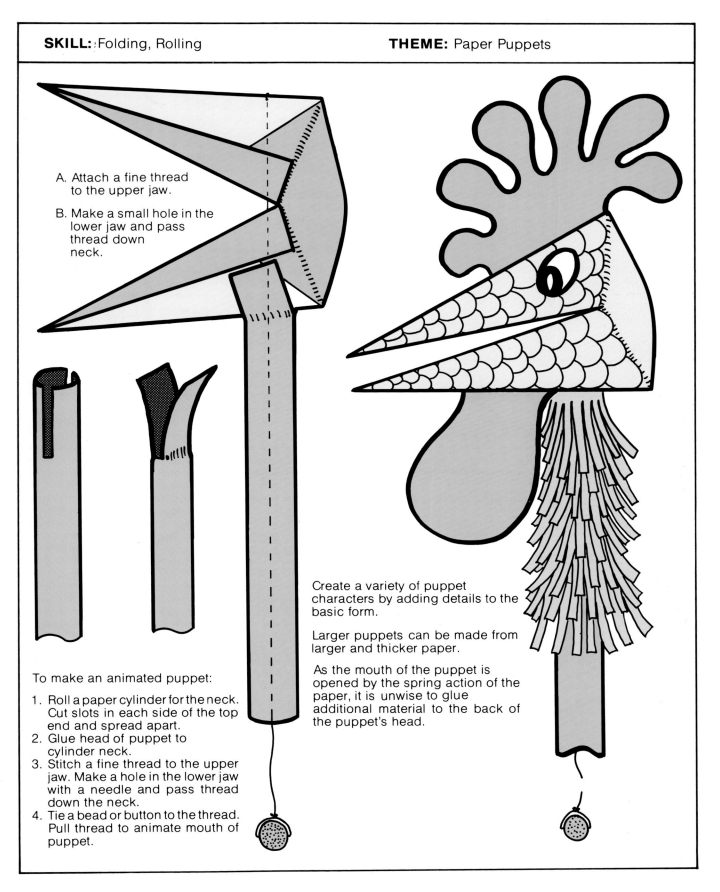

A. Attach a fine thread to the upper jaw.

B. Make a small hole in the lower jaw and pass thread down neck.

Create a variety of puppet characters by adding details to the basic form.

Larger puppets can be made from larger and thicker paper.

As the mouth of the puppet is opened by the spring action of the paper, it is unwise to glue additional material to the back of the puppet's head.

To make an animated puppet:

1. Roll a paper cylinder for the neck. Cut slots in each side of the top end and spread apart.
2. Glue head of puppet to cylinder neck.
3. Stitch a fine thread to the upper jaw. Make a hole in the lower jaw with a needle and pass thread down the neck.
4. Tie a bead or button to the thread. Pull thread to animate mouth of puppet.

The Petshop

I called into the petshop,
To see the petshop man,
"I'm looking for a nice quiet pet,
Please help me if you can".

"Perhaps you'd like a spotted dog,
To play outside the house,
Or would you like a kitten,
A rabbit or a mouse?"

"I think I'll choose a yellow bird,
To whistle when I pass,
But no, ... I'll buy a goldfish,
In a bowl of glass".

THEME: Noah's Ark

The folded puppet, page 46, comes to life when fringed feathers are added.

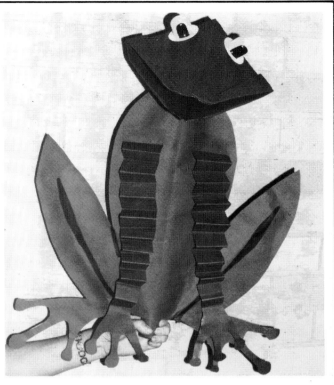

With body shapes glued to each side of the cylinder, and a rounded mouth, a frog results.

Introduce children to primary and secondary colour concepts through a rainbow mobile.

Large, blank wall spaces provide an ideal display area for the flowers on page 78.

- Make individual toothbrushes to display around Leonard.

- Fringe bristles.

- Roll handle.

- Glue together.

Lazy Leonard

Leonard was a lazy lad,
Who seldom cleaned his teeth,
And sad to say his teeth decayed,
On top and underneath.

They ached and gave him dreadful pains,
Which nearly drove him crazy,
So Leonard had to have them out,
All for being lazy.

1. Fold cut mouth.

2. Open out and glue teeth to back surface.

3. Glue the back surface to the face of a Leonard display unit.

4. Make two units - one showing Leonard with healthy teeth and another showing Leonard with broken, missing or discoloured teeth.

Tidy Hair

I looked in the mirror
And to my surprise,
My hair was all ruffled,
Down over my eyes.

I reached for my comb
And I groomed it with care,
So now I am proud
Of my neat tidy hair.

- Cut combs from thin cardboard.

- Fringe the teeth.

- Display combs on a mirror background (foil), with children's drawings of tidy and untidy hair styles.

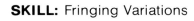

Grain direction of crepe paper

 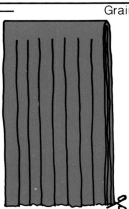 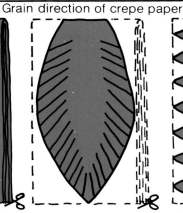 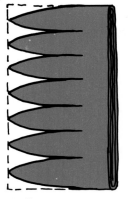 

1. Short fringing along the grain.

2. Long fringing across the grain.

3. Leaf or feather shaped fringing.

4. Pattern or scollop fringing.

5. Double edge fringing.

In each of the above methods, cut a width from a roll of crepe paper. If single pieces are required, cut through the folds at the edge of the width. For leaf or feather fringing, cut the shape first, then fringe the edges. Retain the top fold to support the units. Staple double edge fringing as shown.

Apply various fringing techniques with other paper skills to create some colourful birds.

SKILL: Fringing	**THEME:** Display Ideas

Make some "Cave People". Use fringing to represent their clothes.

Use fringing to represent the thatching of a Pacific Island village.
Three dimensional models can be made from cardboard boxes covered with fringed paper.

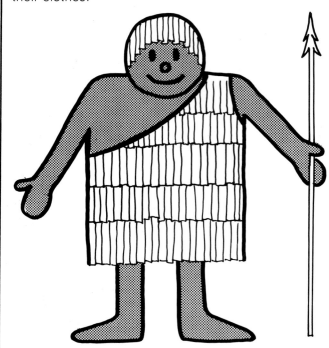

Guinea Pigs

I visited the petshop,
And much to my delight,
I bought a pair of guinea pigs,
With coats of brown and white.

I treated them with loving care,
And soon to my surprise,
I found I had four guinea pigs,
Right before my eyes.

Their home was getting crowded,
So I built a bigger pen,
I'm rather pleased I built it,
Because I now have ten.

My Mum is getting very cross,
I know I'm in a fix,
She counted them the other day,
The total - thirty six!

So now I've made a great big sign,
And hung it on a nail,
I've painted it in brown and white -
GUINEA PIGS FOR SALE.

Prepare a graph to indicate how children prefer their eggs for breakfast.
Cover a cardboard oblong shape with fringing then add comb, wattles, beak and eyes.
Cut these parts from coloured paper and glue to both sides of the fringing.
The graph can be displayed on a two dimensional surface or suspended in the form of a mobile.

MILK CARTON HENS

Use an assortment of clean milk or juice cartons to make these hens.
Scollop some crepe paper as shown, then work from the bottom of the carton up.
Glue each row. Add combs, wattles, beak and eyes.

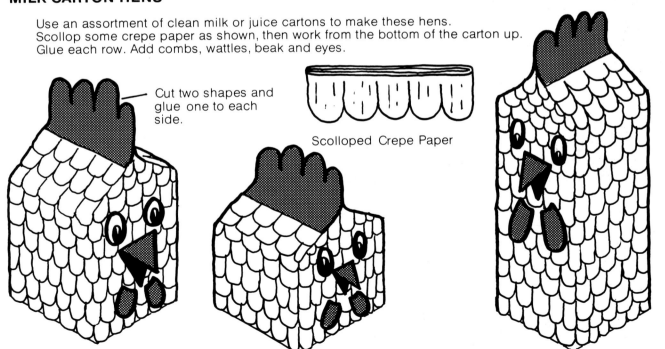

Cut two shapes and glue one to each side.

Scolloped Crepe Paper

We went to St. Mary's High.

They had farm animals there

We had a great time!

We saw some sheep.

We saw some goat

We saw some chickens

aw some turkeys.

We saw some pigs.

Examples of three classroom displays using handwork skills to represent the themes of:
1. An Excursion
2. Doris the Dragon (Ref. page 11)
3. Hickory Dickory Dock.

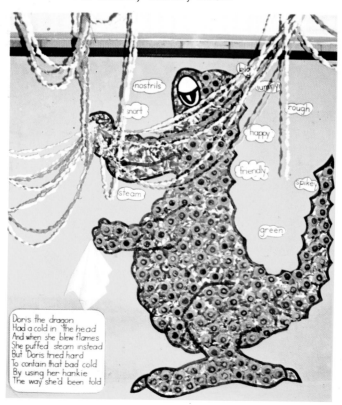

nostrils

snort

happy

friendly

steam

rough

spikey

green

Doris the dragon
Had a cold in the head
And when she blew flames
She puffed steam instead
But Doris tried hard
To contain that bad cold
By using her hankie
The way she'd been told

ABOVE: Using the skills shown on page 57, these Koalas have been displayed amongst clusters of gum leaves. Include vocabulary development material in the display.

BELOW: Cut cheese shapes from yellow paper and display on a dark background.

"The hens are busy laying eggs for tea".

An ideal group activity, the head, wings, body and laying box of each hen can be made by several children, with the various units being brought together to form the final display.

Suggested Size:
Body = 45cm. dia.
Wing = 28cm. dia.
Head = 18cm. dia.
Nest = 15cm. x 50cm.

- Use the basic shapes of circles and semicircles in various combinations to make each hen in her laying box.
- Cover the shapes with fringed crepe paper or circles cut from crepe.
- Fringe some straw to glue to the inside edge of the laying box.
- Print the outside surface of the laying box with foam plastic dipped in paint.

Many handwork activities can be developed by applying strips of fringed crepe paper to shapes cut from thin cardboard. The three dimensional effect of the form will be heightened if the shapes are made into low profile cones. Set out below are the main stages in making a Koala.

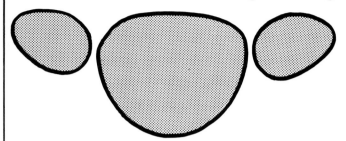

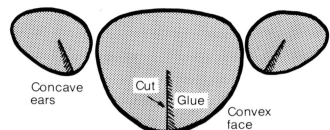

Concave ears   Cut   Glue   Convex face

1. Cut cardboard to shape of face and ears.

2. Make radial cuts shown and overlap to form low profile cones.

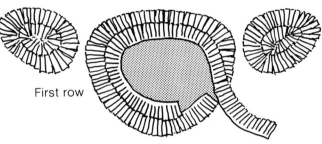

First row

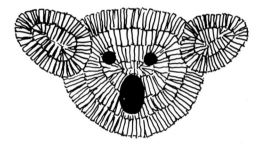

3. Cover cones with fringed grey crepe paper. Work from outside edge towards centre.

4. Glue ears to face. Cut eyes and nose from black paper and glue in position.

Extend the activity shown above by adding bodies to the Koalas and displaying them in a setting of Gum Trees. Leaves may be printed (use cardboard or styrofoam), cut from finger painting, or be a collage of leaves. Trunk areas can be painted or made from bark.

See our Koalas

Bushfires destroy Koalas

Baby Koala is in the pouch.

Koalas are marsupials

Koalas eat gum leaves

Koalas have a coat of soft fur.

SKILL: Fringing, Chipping	**THEME:** The Three Bears

The methods of applying fringed crepe paper to a supportive base can be developed in several ways. As shown on the previous page, the base for the head of the Koala has been cut from flat cardboard which has then been formed into a cone. This procedure adds strength and dimension to the finished model, however other approaches may be more appropriate. Paper plates form an ideal base for many models, but as these incur an unnecessary cost factor, cardboard shapes cut from cardboard cartons for large units, and thin cardboard for small units serve as a satisfactory base.

The ideas which follow can be used in many ways. Small units may be made as individual activities in the form of masks, stick puppets, or as part of a collective class display.
Larger units provide useful group projects for mobiles, murals or standing displays.

Mask

Stick Puppet

father

baby

mother

Make legs from cardboard strips covered with fringing.

How many pigs is the farmer's dog minding?

Apply fringing from outside edge, with subsequent
rows working towards the centre.
Cut facial features as separate units and glue over
fringed area.

Glue ears to
back surface
of circle.

SKILL: Pleating	**THEME:** Developing the Skill

Pleating is simply a series of folds which alternate in direction throughout the length of the paper.

Pleat a slithering snake

or a humping caterpillar.

Use pleating to make a piano accordion.

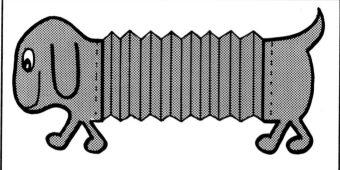

Add a head and tail to a pleated body.

Pleat a hive for busy bees.

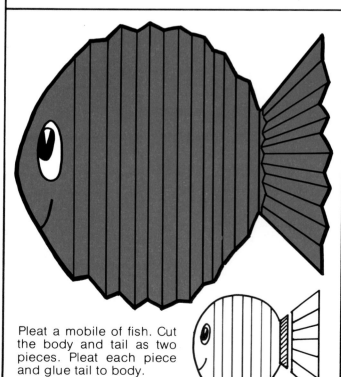

Pleat a mobile of fish. Cut the body and tail as two pieces. Pleat each piece and glue tail to body.

Create some Pleated Paper People. Add heads and legs to wide strips of pleating.

HUNGRY MICE

Thread a piece of wool through the last pleat for the tail.

Make blocks of cheese from cardboard formed into a prism. Paint yellow and add black areas to represent holes.

CHINESE LANTERNS

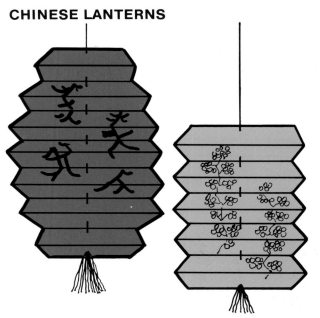

Cut lantern shapes and decorate with Chinese symbols or pictorial forms. Pleat the lanterns and thread wool through the pleats.

CATERPILLARS

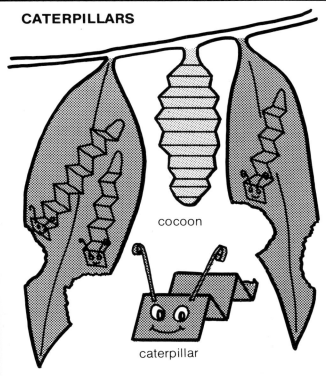

cocoon

caterpillar

Cut leaves from painted paper. Pleat caterpillars from the same colour and relate to the theme of camouflage.

EGG CARTON BIRDS

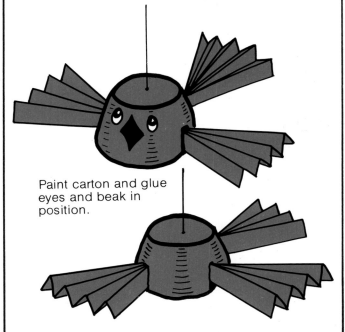

Paint carton and glue eyes and beak in position.

Cut an egg carton into single sections. Pleat wings and tail and glue into slits cut into the egg carton unit.

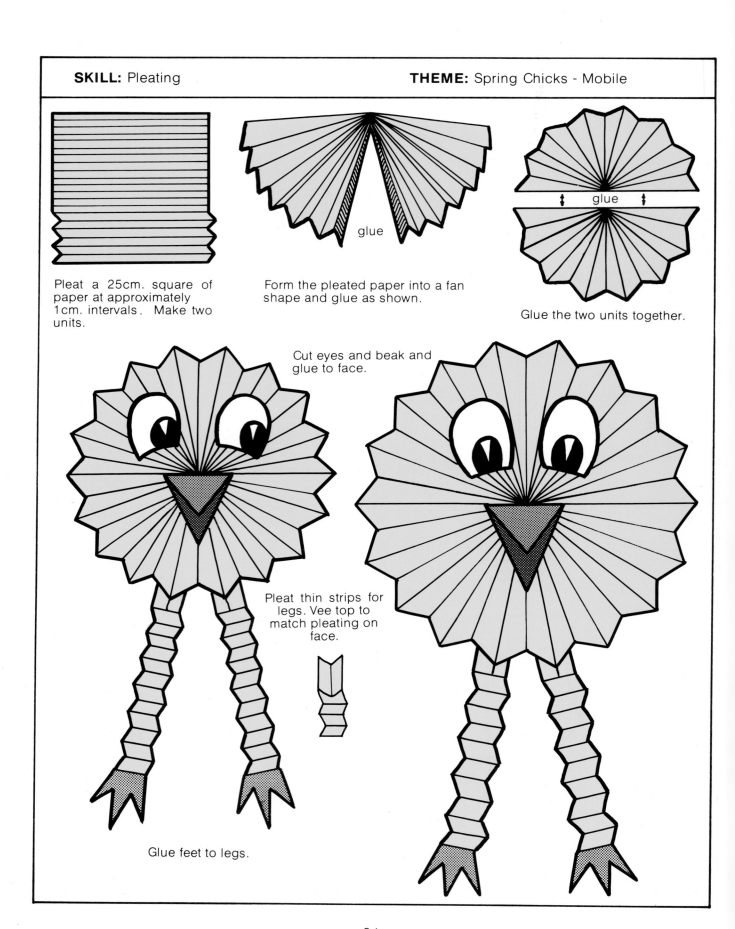

Pleat a 25cm. square of paper at approximately 1cm. intervals. Make two units.

Form the pleated paper into a fan shape and glue as shown.

Glue the two units together.

Cut eyes and beak and glue to face.

Pleat thin strips for legs. Vee top to match pleating on face.

Glue feet to legs.

1. Fold cut symmetrical body.

2. Cut shapes for forefeet and hind feet.

3. Pleat strips of paper or thin cardboard to represent forelegs and hind legs.
Attach feet, and glue to body of frog.

4. Cut shapes for eggs.

Enlarge scale to suit display area.

5. Cut outline of tadpole. Pleat tail.

6. Prepare a "Frog Life Cycle" mural.

"Spring Chicks". This effective mobile has been made by suspending a number of the pleated chicks, ref. page 64, on threads of varying length.

a Poultry Farm display. Combine a number of the units shown on page 56 to form an Egg Production Shed.

An Autumn tree brings a colourful display to the classroom.

Add colourful eggs to folded rabbits to make an Easter Mobile.

A bowl of Easter daisies makes an attractive Easter display.

Springtime is shearing time for these curled paper sheep. Ref. page 26.

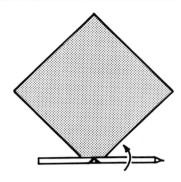
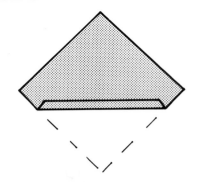
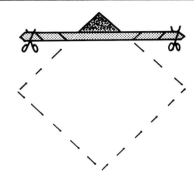

1. When rolling cylinders from thin material, e.g. paper, use a pencil to help form the cylinder.

2. Start from one corner and roll towards the opposite corner. Remove the pencil before it is rolled into the cylinder.

3. Glue the opposite corner to prevent the cylinder from unrolling. Trim each end if required.

Insert crepe paper flames.

Make a large cardboard cake. Fringe a trim and roll candles to celebrate a special birthday.

Build a nest of rolled paper twigs. Make some cotton ball chicks.

Make a giant Echidna. Paint the background shape and cover it with rolled paper spikes.

Echidna

When it's time for dinner
Echidna has a treat,
He swiftly flicks his long
              tongue out
And picks up ants to eat.

Tree trunks

Sun

Spikes of fish

Goal Posts

Cocoon

Signs

Traffic Lights

Flag Poles.

Ship's Masts.

Dragon's Teeth.

Fireworks

Cut wings from cardboard.

Beads - Roll thin strips

Sheeps' legs.

Fence Posts.

Roll cylinders to make a model plane or rocket.

The Witches Broom

Stems for flowers.   Make window box from scrap styrofoam.

ABOVE: A follow-up activity based on an excursion to a Fishermen's Co-operative. Individual paintings of the people on the wharf provide scope for the whole class to contribute. The remainder of the unit has been prepared by small groups working on: city backdrop, fishing trawler, water and birds. A small paint roller was used to produce the wave effect on the water.

BELOW: Extending the "Fishing" theme, a range of painting and printing techniques has been used in this group project.

Large painted leaves, cut to their outline, form this colourful Autumn tree.

Language development can be facilitated through handwork activities.

A variety of clean milk cartons has been used to make this poultry farm. Ref. page 53.

SKILL: Rolling, Folding, Fringing, Chipping **THEME:** Springtime

Springtime

Days a little warmer,
Trees shoot leaves of green,
Baby chicks are hatching,
Springtime paints the scene.

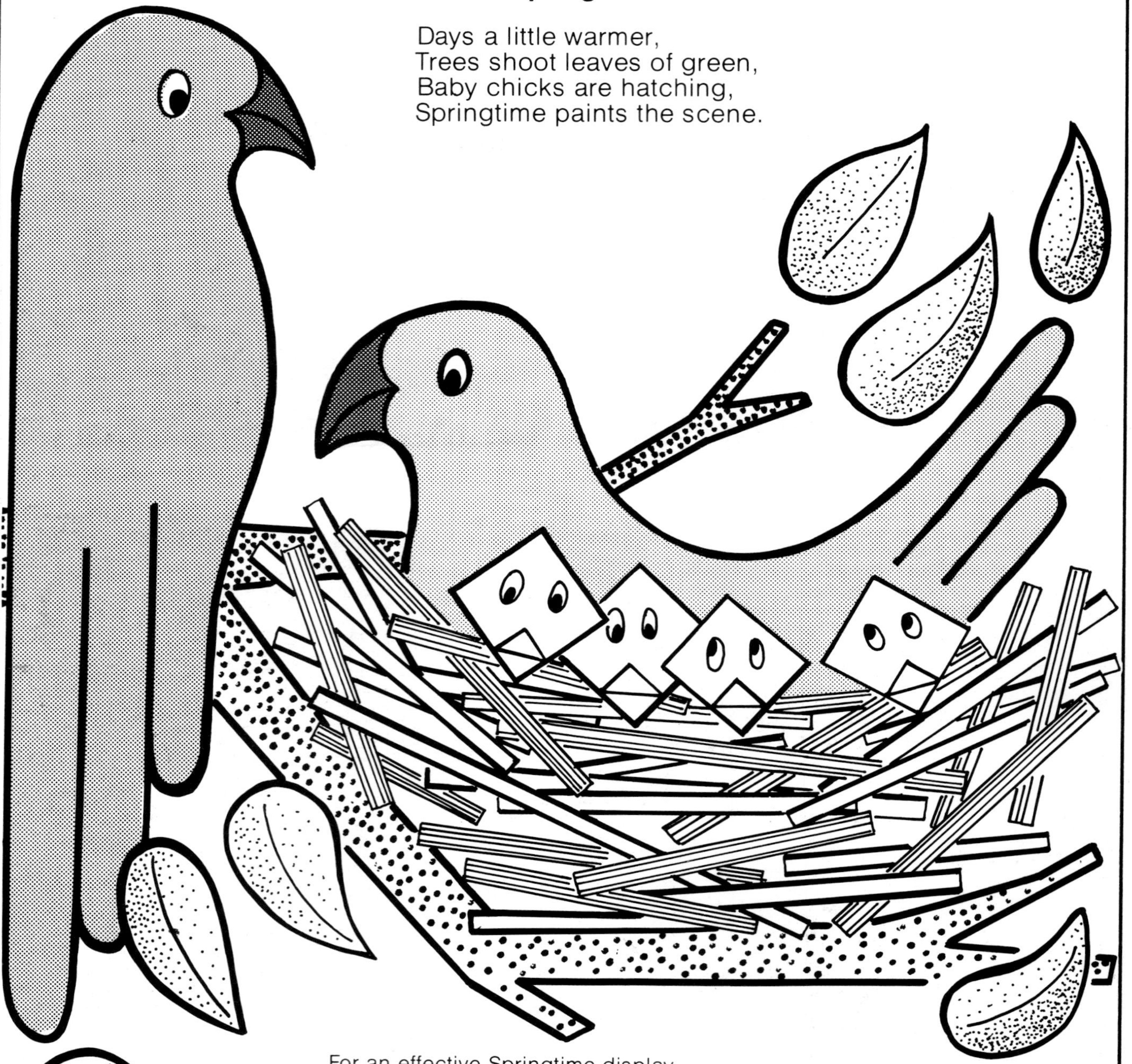

For an effective Springtime display -

- Paint or finger paint a large light blue background.
- Paint or apply cut out shapes for branches.
- Cut bird shapes from cardboard and apply skills.
- Roll magazine pages into "twigs" for nest.
- Finger paint and cut out leaves.
- Fold baby chicks.

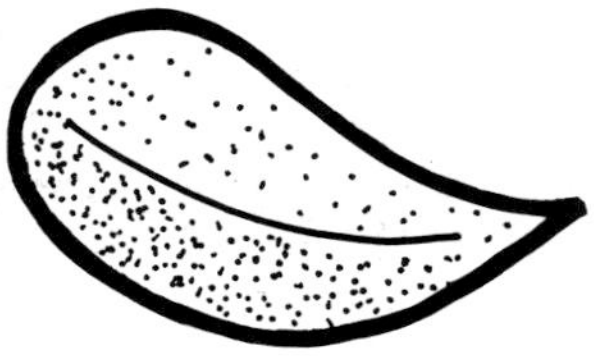

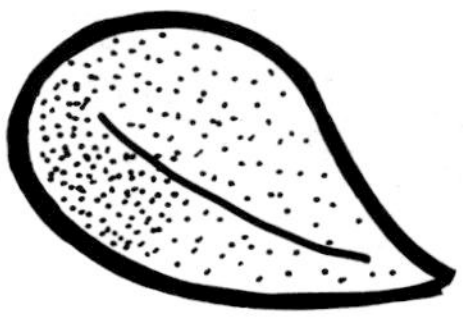

A bowl of cellophane filled flowers makes a striking window display.

Paper curls on cardboard cylinders form the Santas on this festive mobile.

These round faced Santas reflect the individuality of their creators. Suspended across the classroom, they make a cheerful Christmas decoration.

wharf
ferry
pilot station
rocks
Nobbys
harbour
breakwater
tug boat
trawler
water
bulk carrier
signal station
ships
cargo
cranes
industry
chimney
pollution
funnel
silos
dock
city

The men at the signal station direct ships into the harbour and measure the wind, rainfall and temperature.

Our Busy Harbour

The breakwater is made of very large rocks.

The pilot station is important to the harbour.

When you come to visit our city by ship the first thing you will see will be the harbour area.

An excursion provides children with a range of ideas and information which can be incorporated in follow-up craft activities.

The tug boat helps to guide the ships safely into the harbour.

FULLERTON COVE

Combine the children's own drawings with other skills in creating activities which reflect important aspects of the excursion.

Many excursions involve some type of transport which can form the basis for one aspect of the follow-up activities.

The refrigerated trays in this display have been made from foil covered boxes filled with styrofoam pieces. Notice how the expanded paper net links the two activities.

The soft edge of torn paper frequently is more appropriate to an activity than the hard edge produced by cutting. Paper tearing is an excellent means of developing fine motor control and hand-eye coordination. The actual skill is achieved by placing the thumb and index finger of each hand on either side of the line to be torn, then tearing only the area between the thumbs. By repeating this process the length and direction of each tear can be accurately controlled. Tearing can follow an outline or produce random shapes of colour and texture, which can be used to represent a wide range of ideas.

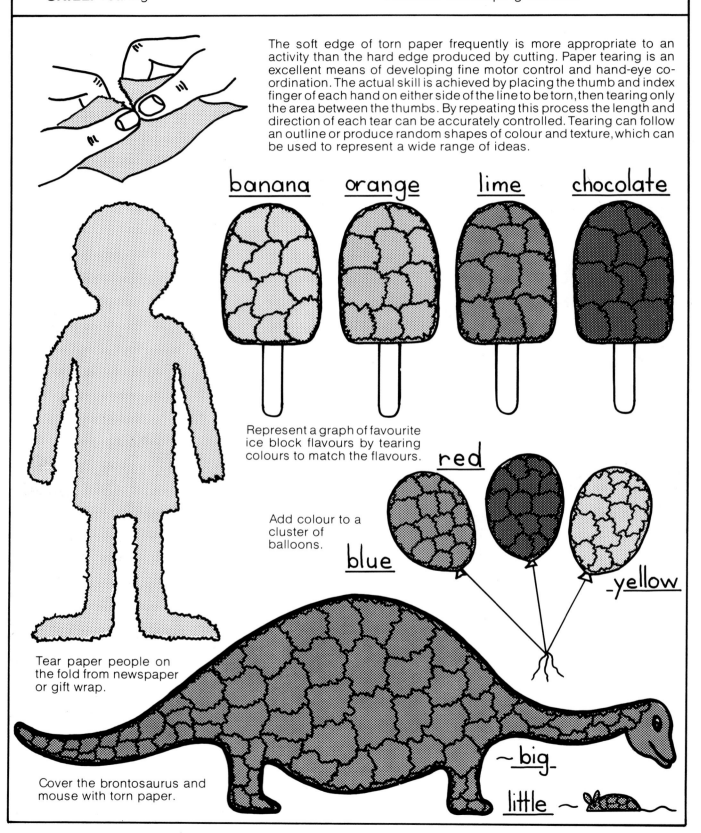

banana   orange   lime   chocolate

Represent a graph of favourite ice block flavours by tearing colours to match the flavours.

Add colour to a cluster of balloons.

red

blue

yellow

Tear paper people on the fold from newspaper or gift wrap.

~big~

little ~

Cover the brontosaurus and mouse with torn paper.

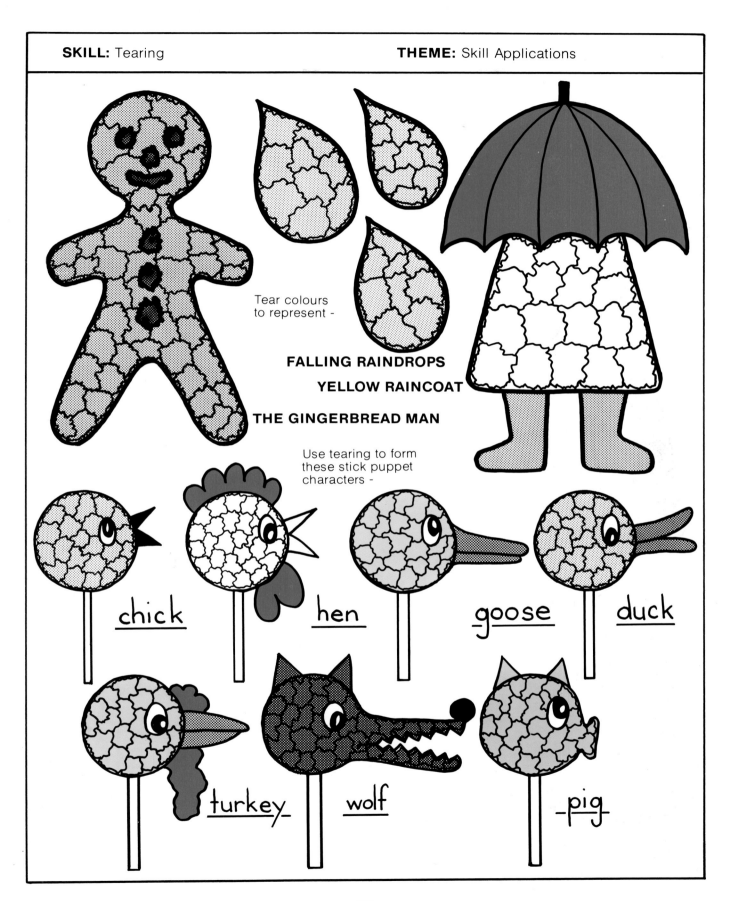

Tear colours
to represent -

FALLING RAINDROPS

YELLOW RAINCOAT

THE GINGERBREAD MAN

Use tearing to form
these stick puppet
characters -

chick hen goose duck

turkey wolf pig

77

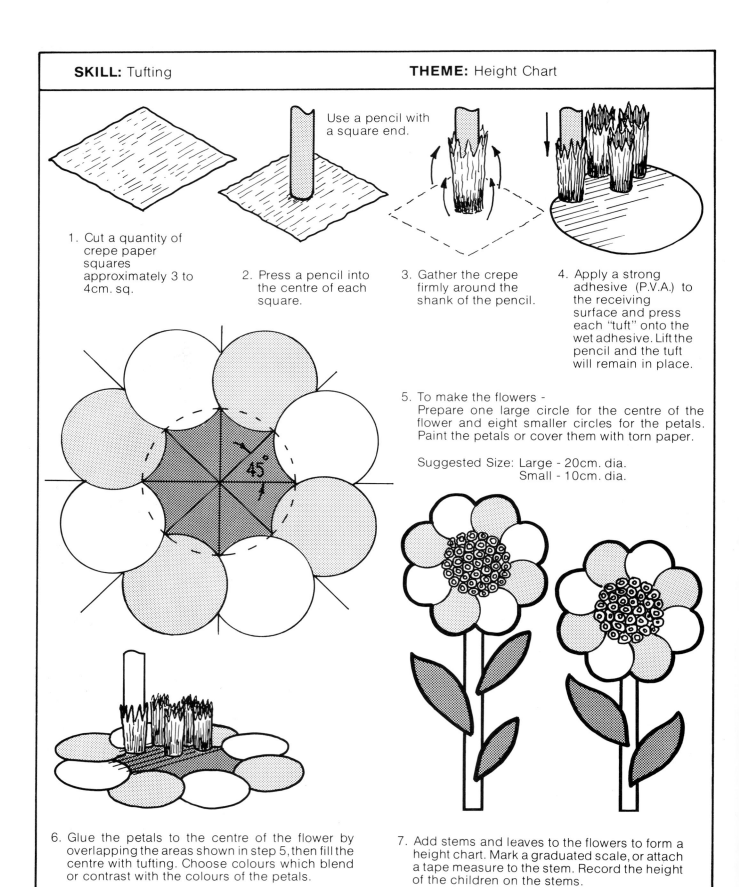

Use a pencil with a square end.

1. Cut a quantity of crepe paper squares approximately 3 to 4cm. sq.

2. Press a pencil into the centre of each square.

3. Gather the crepe firmly around the shank of the pencil.

4. Apply a strong adhesive (P.V.A.) to the receiving surface and press each "tuft" onto the wet adhesive. Lift the pencil and the tuft will remain in place.

5. To make the flowers – Prepare one large circle for the centre of the flower and eight smaller circles for the petals. Paint the petals or cover them with torn paper.

   Suggested Size: Large - 20cm. dia.
   Small - 10cm. dia.

45°

6. Glue the petals to the centre of the flower by overlapping the areas shown in step 5, then fill the centre with tufting. Choose colours which blend or contrast with the colours of the petals.

7. Add stems and leaves to the flowers to form a height chart. Mark a graduated scale, or attach a tape measure to the stem. Record the height of the children on the stems.

78

Tuft larger squares of crepe to represent the foliage of trees.

Use tufting to represent the wool on sheep and spring lambs.

On a horizontal surface, use tufting to represent grass, vegetable crops or by using coloured crepe paper, represent beds of gaily coloured flowers.

Trees

Trees are the kindest plants I know,
They do no harm, they simply grow.
And offer birds a bough to nest,
Or spread some shade for sheep to rest.

In Springtime, trees with blossoms gay,
Add some colour to each day,
Then, bearing fruit that's ripe and sweet,
Bring to all a Summer treat.

Their Autumn leaves, gold and brown,
Form a carpet on the ground
And when cold winter days are nigh,
Their leafless branches reach the sky.

So why not help their numbers grow?
Find a place where you can sow
A tiny seedling, straight and free
Then, tend it as it grows - a tree.

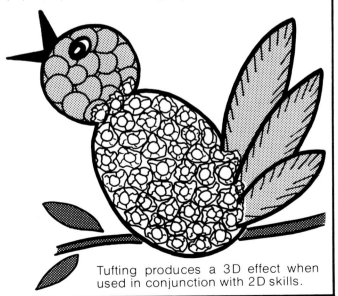

Tufting produces a 3D effect when used in conjunction with 2D skills.

Based on the skill of fold cutting, Santa can be made to any size. Small units make an attractive mobile while larger units feature as a central display. If Santa is to be viewed from both sides, make two units and glue them back-to-back.

To make Santa -
- Fold cut body shape.
- Trim "spare" hat area.
- Paint face, hands, suit, boots.
- Add tufting for beard and trim.
- Glue on eyes, nose, moustache, belt.

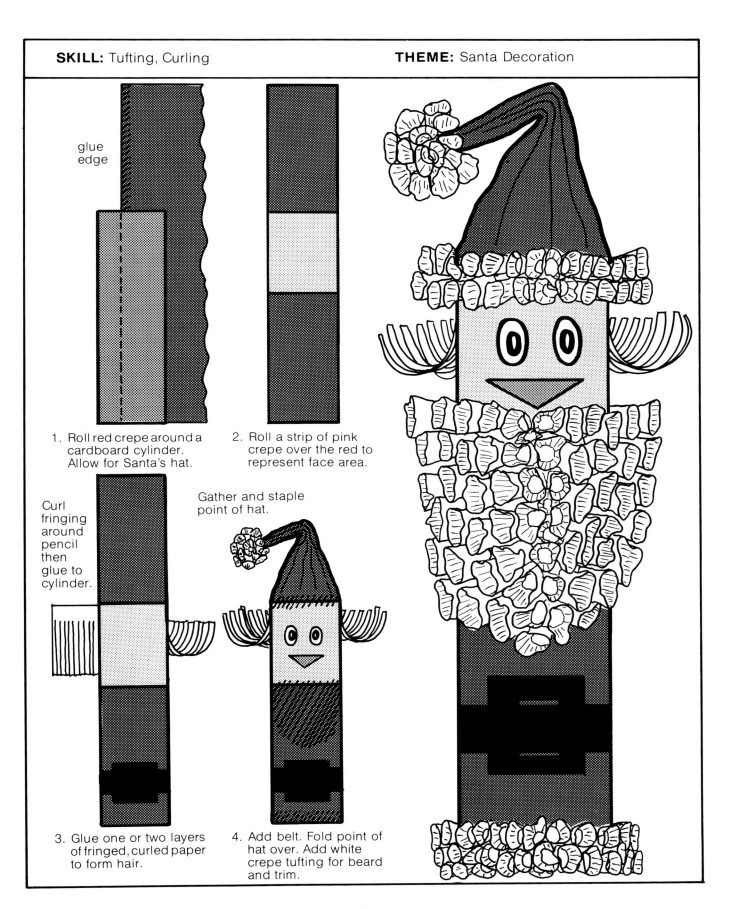

glue edge

1. Roll red crepe around a cardboard cylinder. Allow for Santa's hat.

2. Roll a strip of pink crepe over the red to represent face area.

Curl fringing around pencil then glue to cylinder.

Gather and staple point of hat.

3. Glue one or two layers of fringed, curled paper to form hair.

4. Add belt. Fold point of hat over. Add white crepe tufting for beard and trim.

Honey Bees

I saw a hive of honey bees
With brown and amber wings,
Buzzing in the springtime warmth
That mid September brings.

They danced among the flowers
Like children at their play,
Then quickly spread their fragile wings
And softly flew away.

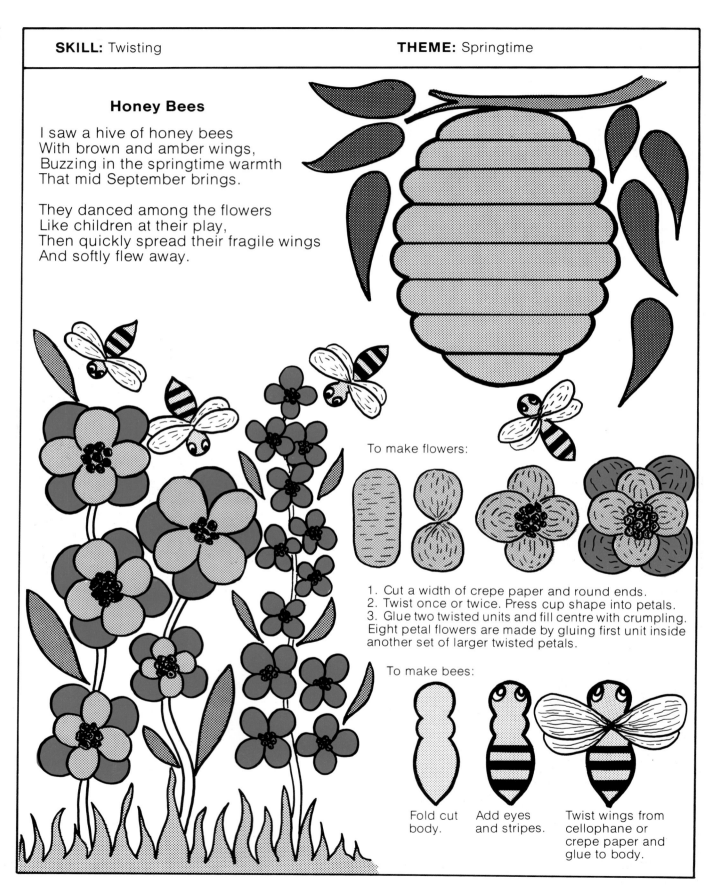

To make flowers:

1. Cut a width of crepe paper and round ends.
2. Twist once or twice. Press cup shape into petals.
3. Glue two twisted units and fill centre with crumpling.
Eight petal flowers are made by gluing first unit inside
another set of larger twisted petals.

To make bees:

Fold cut
body.

Add eyes
and stripes.

Twist wings from
cellophane or
crepe paper and
glue to body.

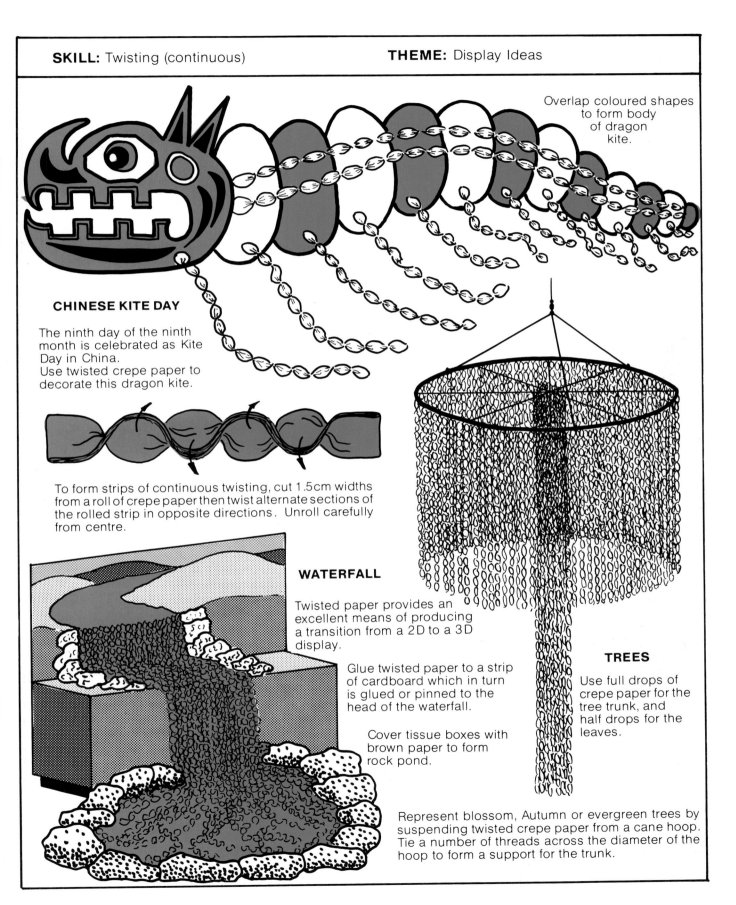

Overlap coloured shapes
to form body
of dragon
kite.

CHINESE KITE DAY

The ninth day of the ninth
month is celebrated as Kite
Day in China.
Use twisted crepe paper to
decorate this dragon kite.

To form strips of continuous twisting, cut 1.5cm widths
from a roll of crepe paper then twist alternate sections of
the rolled strip in opposite directions. Unroll carefully
from centre.

WATERFALL

Twisted paper provides an
excellent means of producing
a transition from a 2D to a 3D
display.

Glue twisted paper to a strip
of cardboard which in turn
is glued or pinned to the
head of the waterfall.

Cover tissue boxes with
brown paper to form
rock pond.

TREES

Use full drops of
crepe paper for the
tree trunk, and
half drops for the
leaves.

Represent blossom, Autumn or evergreen trees by
suspending twisted crepe paper from a cane hoop.
Tie a number of threads across the diameter of the
hoop to form a support for the trunk.

WEAVING MATS

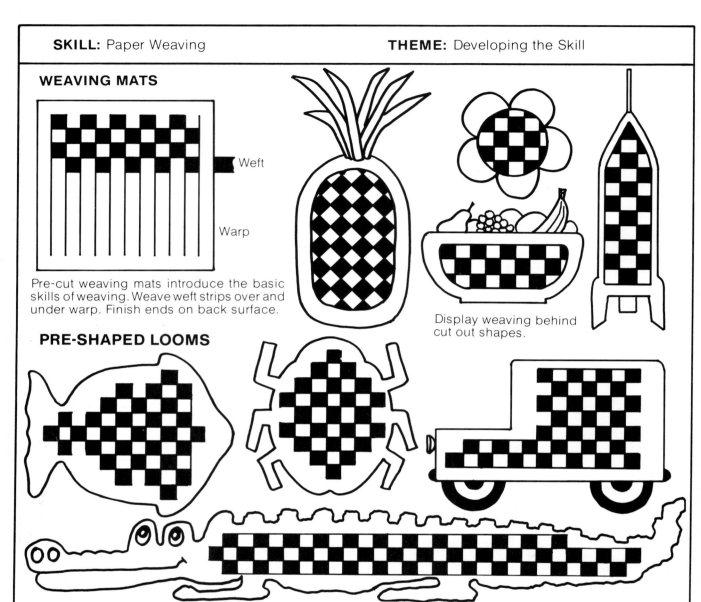

Pre-cut weaving mats introduce the basic skills of weaving. Weave weft strips over and under warp. Finish ends on back surface.

Display weaving behind cut out shapes.

PRE-SHAPED LOOMS

With this form of weaving, the warp is actually cut into the shape. Weft strips are then woven to make the pattern. Finish ends on back surface.

FREE FORM LOOMS

Warp and weft strips are curved in free form looms. Finish ends on back surface.

Free form weaving makes an effective background for other types of display. Notice how the bottom weft strip is tapered, rather than curved to facilitate its placement in the warp.

Which part of the plant do we eat?

Brussel sprouts
Spinach
lettuce chives
cabbage
Leaves
Tubers and Roots
radishes
carrots
turnip
potatoes
corn
peanuts
peas
seeds
Fruit
pumpkin
grapes
peach
Flowe
bro
aspa
Shoots and Bulbs

ABOVE: Which Part of the Plant Do We Eat?

LEFT: Weaving was used to make the large and small soup pots in the Vegetable Soup display.

BELOW: Children in a Kindergarten class have used weaving to make the Ridiculous Robots.

peas
beans
cauliflower
parsnips
turnip
tomatoes
celery
carrots
onions
potatoes
We made some vegetable soup

ridiculous
robots
oats.

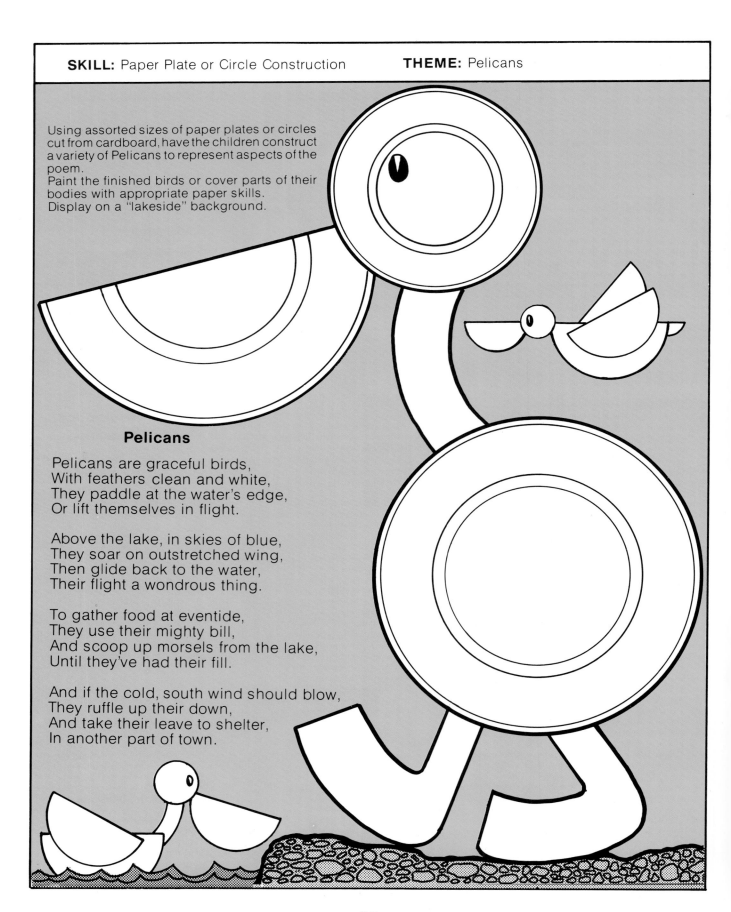

SKILL: Paper Plate or Circle Construction   **THEME:** Pelicans

Using assorted sizes of paper plates or circles cut from cardboard, have the children construct a variety of Pelicans to represent aspects of the poem.
Paint the finished birds or cover parts of their bodies with appropriate paper skills.
Display on a "lakeside" background.

Pelicans

Pelicans are graceful birds,
With feathers clean and white,
They paddle at the water's edge,
Or lift themselves in flight.

Above the lake, in skies of blue,
They soar on outstretched wing,
Then glide back to the water,
Their flight a wondrous thing.

To gather food at eventide,
They use their mighty bill,
And scoop up morsels from the lake,
Until they've had their fill.

And if the cold, south wind should blow,
They ruffle up their down,
And take their leave to shelter,
In another part of town.

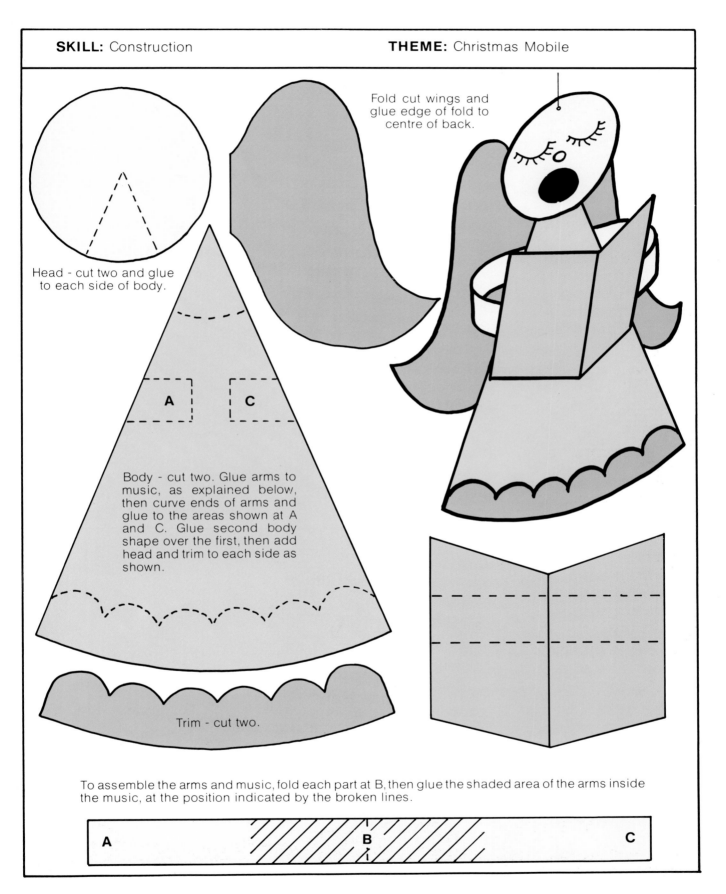

Fold cut wings and glue edge of fold to centre of back.

Head - cut two and glue to each side of body.

Body - cut two. Glue arms to music, as explained below, then curve ends of arms and glue to the areas shown at A and C. Glue second body shape over the first, then add head and trim to each side as shown.

Trim - cut two.

To assemble the arms and music, fold each part at B, then glue the shaded area of the arms inside the music, at the position indicated by the broken lines.

A   B   C

The Helpful Dragon

Dragon is a friendly chap,
With coat of emerald green,
He seldom roars or belches fire,
Unless he's feeling mean.

He'll help you with your spelling,
A service he gives free,
But if you do not learn the words,
He'll eat you for his tea.